Praise for
Struggle to Strength

Author, Kip Shubert, reminds us that by reflecting on the ingredients that life's lessons give us, we can use those challenges to embrace our vulnerability and use them to our advantage. *Struggle to Strength* is a story of Kip's journey through the toughest times; including addiction, divorce, financial failures, and health issues, and how he found the secret sauce to a healthier way of living – relationships!

Jimmy Casas
Leadership Coach, Educator, Author, Speaker

I absolutely love when people unleash the power of vulnerability! Kip does exactly this in his book *Struggle to Strength*. Kip is a miracle! I'm not sure there is any other way to describe him. In his book he lays it all on the line as to how he is a miracle, and in fact, everyone is! If you have a deep love for people and want to experience true joy, Kip's book will make your day! It will also help you keep an eye out for potential "Kips" in your life, in your classroom if you're an educator, and possibly another co-worker who is struggling and is a miracle in waiting.

Steve Woolf
Wild Heart Teacher, Founder, Director

Struggle to Strength is the ultimate redemption story. What stood out to me was that change didn't simply occur by Kip looking in the mirror and choosing change. Kip's life changed when he was able to look past himself and see all of the people behind him in that mirror whose lives were impacted by him. I am one of those people. His resurgence has given me strength and optimism, and for that, I am extremely grateful. I truly admire the transparency that Kip uses to give a sneak peak into his struggles that lead him to a place of despair. I appreciate him allowing readers an authentic experience as he shares stories that, I can only imagine, were difficult to put into words. Thank you, Kip, proud to call you my friend.

Eddie Wright
Director of District Athletics
Oklahoma City Public Schools

I am so proud of my son for the humble and genuine authenticity of his book. His words are inspiring and encouraging. God is using Kip to reach hundreds of students and people. What God has brought him through is a miracle, and I always knew that He had special plans for Kip's life. My prayer for you, as you read this book, is that you will come to believe that you are a miracle and find the purpose for your life that God has planned. I love you son.

Ed Shubert
Dad

Kip Shubert's book is a great testimony to the incredible lessons he has learned as a sober father, teacher and coach. *Struggle to Strength* is a great read. It is fast and deep. I appreciated how the chapters centered around a single piece of wisdom. Sometimes, the chapters could be summarized by a simple object or phrase, such as a giant stuffed animal or "Try harder, Daddy." Those simple concepts resonate in a profound way for the readers. Shubert delves to incredible depths, and he possesses the courage to bring readers there with him. Read his book, and you will find yourself in the presence of one of those rare inspirational teachers who changes the trajectory of your life.

Mark Goodson
Teacher

Kip chronicles his journey through a series of trials and adversities, which were gut-wrenching and heartbreaking to read. Yet, through it all, he NEVER gives up hope and ultimately finds healing and restoration through his faith, his determination to forgive himself, and his deep love that exceeds all boundaries. From the very first page, his words drew me in as he visually painted a story that took me from a place of harsh abandonment to humble redemption. Kip's genuine vulnerability makes his story incredibly relatable. Every reader will come to understand the pain and joy that Kip has experienced and will be inspired by his strength and resilience.

Jillian Dubois
Redesigned Educator, Author, Illustrator

Struggle to Strength: Finding the Ingredients to Your Secret Sauce, by Kip Shubert, is an inspirational story about one educator's journey from rock bottom to the top again. Any educator could relate to this story filled with trials and tribulations, personally and professionally.

Kip's story shares how he navigated learning to rebuild relationship skills that had been broken by relationship trauma. He shares tips on how to be aware of when to ask for help and believing in your heart that you CAN and WILL overcome. "If we truly want to be that greatest miracle in the world in all we do, it starts with meeting ourselves where we are and loving who we are right now," Kip states. This story is truly motivational!

Ashley Hubner
Instructional Coach & Curriculum Specialist

Struggle To Strength is an authentic story about making adversity your advantage. This book is filled with raw vulnerability and is a must read for educators and all who need to grow from their challenges. Read this book and keep climbing!

Jon Gordon
14x best-selling author of The Energy Bus *and* The One Truth

Each of us is on our own journey. We make decisions daily about whether we are going to take a meandering stroll or if we are going to walk with a purpose. The point is that we need to be intentional about the path that we are walking. In *Struggle to Strength*, Kip Shubert helps you find your own secret sauce that will aid you in mapping out your own course if you are willing to fail forward and own your epic. Through intense self-reflection and vulnerability, Kip shows that a fallible person can still make good and have a huge impact on others if they are willing to take a hard look at themselves in the mirror.

Jay Dostal, Ed.D
Father, Author of #OwnYourEpic, Educator,
2016 NE Principal of the Year
2021 AR Principal of the Year

When I first began reading Kip's story, I had a bit of background knowledge on his journey and story. Little did I know the depth and complexity of its wholeness. Kip goes deep into his past, his troubles, his successes, and displays a pure vulnerability that not many have shown. Drinking, depression, facing death and despair, blooming where we are planted, all bring a familiar tingle to my heart and brain. I am so blessed and grateful to have read this heart-capturing journey, and will definitely refer to it often, share it, and hope that the world will embark upon the journey too. Kip brings it. He brings it all the way, my friends!

Jeff Kubiak
Equity Educator, Author, Speaker

Life is full of adversity; the challenge comes with how we react when adversity comes our way. In *Struggle to Strength: Finding the Ingredients to Your Secret Sauce*, Kip shares a powerful testimony around his personal journey of life. Real, authentic, and emotional, this book is a reflection of the fact that you can't have a testimony without a test. Kip's willingness to share his vulnerabilities are a reflection of who he has become, not only as an educator, but as a human being. You will laugh, you will cry, and most importantly, you will reflect on the greatest belief that each of us can have: hope for a better tomorrow.

Phil Campbell
Speaker, Author, Consultant

Struggle to Strength: Finding the Ingredients to Your Secret Sauce

Copyright © by Kip Shubert
First Edition 2023

All rights reserved.

No part of this publication may be reproduced in any form, or by any means, electronic or mechanical, including photocopying, recording, or any information browsing, storage or retrieval system, without permission in writing from the publisher.

Cover photo credit to Cynthia Shubert Photography

Road to Awesome, LLC.

*To my amazing children:
Haley, Blake, Brady, and Kamdyn.*

This book is dedicated to you. You are resilient warriors who became the victims of my struggle. Yet, you are the driving force behind my determination to keep climbing. My strength today is due to your presence in my life. I hope this book honors you always.

*Love you,
Dad*

Table of Contents

Foreward — 1

Introduction — 5

Chapter 1 — 9
I think you should wear something nice.

Chapter 2 — 15
Try harder, Daddy,

Chapter 3 — 25
Rock Bottom to Recovery

Chapter 4 — 35
A Giant Stuffed Animal

Chapter 5 — 43
It is what it is.

Chapter 6 — 51
Getting My Daughter Back

Chapter 7 — 61
A Warrior's Mindset

Chapter 8 — 69
The Gift of Grace

Chapter 9 — 77
Reaching Back Over the Mountain

Chapter 10 — 87
Dream big, so big they will call you crazy.

Conclusion — 97

Acknowledgements — 103

About the Author — 107

FOREWARD

Dr. Brandon Beck
Teacher, Speaker, Author, Coach, Podcast Host

Very few people survive rock-bottom and live to tell the story. Even fewer people recover, grow, and live to share their lessons in today's schools with educators and students. Kip Shubert's story is a testimony encouraging you to reach down within your soul to define who you really want to be. *Struggle to Strength* is an inspirational narrative describing his journey from homeless alcoholic to thriving educator and award winning coach. It is about how our pain is our superpower, how our challenges are instrumental for growth. And it is a story about how often our growth is met with limitations and negative beliefs that try to get in the way of our progress.

I first met Kip in 2020. We are both soccer coaches, teachers, and speakers serving students to unlock their unlimited potential on the road to awesome. I didn't know it at the time, but this connection would turn into an opportunity to be alongside him as he would grind, dream, and develop this book from beginning to end. As one of his results coaches, it is incredibly rewarding to see that his story is finally going to be shared with the world. This story will make you laugh, cry, and ponder how you can make deeper connections with those you serve.

Kip's coaching achievements go far beyond awards or certificates. As a successful coach, developing connections, culture, and student leadership is at the forefront of Kip's priorities. In each chapter, Kip teaches you to turn your fears into your fuel, to lead with your focus on service, and to reach back over that mountain time and time again. As the going gets tough, he prepares students to take on the adversities that lie ahead.

His words are a timely reminder that we are all human and that our flaws do not define us but guide us when we choose to live with a warrior's mindset. Behind the scenes, every single individual experiences bad days, anxiety, loss, and so many other negative forces that try to shackle their performance and productivity. Kip's ingredients to the secret sauce are essential not only for being a better educator, but for living a more purposeful life every single day. He shows us how to fight our way through the sucker punches, battle adversity, embrace the process, and utilize self-love to become a better educator each and every day.

As you read this book, realize that it took immense courage for Kip to share this story. He doesn't leave out details because he is paying it forward so you can learn from his lessons. He takes the lessons learned from traveling this journey through recovery and uses them to teach others to lead with faith and positivity.

In Alcoholics Anonymous, the first line of the Serenity Prayer is, "God, grant me the serenity to accept the things I cannot change." Kip fully embraces this line and uses his story to support and guide others. It is our pasts which make us most qualified to help those around us.

Embrace the power of your story, unleash the power of your future, and let Kip guide you with his wisdom and experience.

Get ready to learn more about your secret sauce!

INTRODUCTION

For over 25 years, I have been told my greatest strengths as a teacher and coach were my abilities to develop life-changing relationships and authentically connect with my students and players. I have never been great with all the new instructional strategies taught in professional development training each year. Heck, I would still rather have my overhead projector, transparencies, and a wet cloth than my smart board. (Who likes a device that makes you feel like you have a single-digit IQ?) I did not believe I was good at many of the things that go into being an effective teacher. I knew the pedagogy of teaching was a weakness of mine, but I was not completely convinced that building relationships was my signature move. I lacked confidence. At one point, I was clinging to what hope I had left in my personal life, and I doubted my ability to connect with myself. I often wondered if I even mattered.

In 2014, that all changed when the value of relationships and self-worth found me. I was desperate to try to hang on to my life while in a rehab facility for addiction and alcoholism. The facility was in a small town in central Oklahoma. So, I had the choice to get sober or blow away with the tumbleweeds I saw rolling across the road as I stared out my window. I wanted to *live*, not die. Dreams of being a better man, father, and friend seemed like a real possibility. For the first time in 46 years, I began to believe in myself again. I was being resurrected by the life-giving spirit of real, honest, and authentic relationships. Recovery saved my life, without a doubt, but it did more than that. It opened up my soul to the knowledge that I mattered and, more importantly, why I mattered. I had a God-given gift. No, it wasn't the ability to drink you under the table. It was to impact people through my ability to connect and develop relationships. I had found my purpose.

I've been to hell and back multiple times with a devastating divorce, deadly addiction, a three-and-a-half-year battle to regain custody of my baby girl, and my wife being diagnosed with an incurable, rare blood cancer. Through these struggles, I found my strength. My adversity became my advantage, and this was how I began to learn about the powerful ingredients in my unique secret sauce. A secret sauce that guided me from rock bottom to become an intentional relationship builder. Not only was this a game changer for me but for my students and staff as well.

I want to share the life experiences I have had that led me to develop lasting relationships and cultures. In your school, your classrooms, and your locker rooms are students and staff who are longing for positive, uplifting relationships. I think we have been following the path to success in education in a backward manner. We have become fixated on results. We chase the newest instructional methods. We focus on data-data-data and higher test scores. Yet we find ourselves further away from the intended target: students with big dreams and loads of unlimited potential. I found the secret sauce to get them there, and I want to share it with you so we can impact the culture of your school and community.

CHAPTER ONE
I think you should wear something nice.

It was just a normal school day. I was up at 5:30 am, doing the half-asleep shuffle to the coffee maker for my morning wake-up call. As my first cup of coffee was brewing I grabbed my journal, my bible, and a pen. The Keurig screeched, signaling my coffee was ready. I sat down at the kitchen table to read, reflect, and write. I began this routine during my recovery from alcoholism, and it has now become how I supercharge my day. This day began with me saying, "I get to…" go make a difference today. But what seemed like a regular day ahead would become one of the most defining days of my life.

Finishing getting ready in our bathroom, I could hear the covers rustle as my wife got out of bed. She met me outside of our bathroom with an odd piece of advice. I was wearing jeans and one of my really comfortable hoodies (you know – the ones with a spaghetti stain here and there and several thousand miles of wear and tear). She stopped me and said, "I think you should wear something nice. At least put on a button down; it will look so much better." Not one to question the wise advice of such a wonderful woman, I changed, kissed her, grabbed my things, and headed out the door. Little did I know, she was in on what that morning would become: the day I would start to realize what my secret sauce was all about.

Pulling into the parking lot at Will Rogers High School was as normal as normal could be. It was a Wednesday, which meant a PLC meeting and planning time. I had plenty to get ready for with the upcoming socratic seminar on China and the building of the Three Gorges Dam. After meeting with my PLC team first thing, I went back to my classroom to begin planning. After about thirty minutes of trying to compose a plan for the next week that would knock the socks off my seventh graders, one of the greatest teachers I have ever taught alongside came into my room. Ann Eichenberger, the other seventh-grade social studies teacher, asked me to accompany her to the English teacher's room next door. I thought nothing of this and followed her. But when she opened the door and ushered me into that classroom, I was sure that somehow I was in big trouble.

Stepping into the room, I saw our district superintendent, a cameraman, a guy from the local news program holding a microphone, and a classroom full of my kids. My first thought was this can't be good. I had been living the best I knew how. I had almost two years of recovery under my belt. The rules and routines were something I now followed. So, what from my past was coming back to haunt me now? I wanted to bolt, but didn't think that would be a good look on the five o'clock news. It was instantly warm in that room; however, my body began to shake as if it were ten below. Our superintendent, Dr. Deborah Gist, began to speak, but I don't remember a word she said.

As the light from the news camera blinded me, I turned to look back into the classroom. There stood my wife, my mom and dad, my sister and brother, my babysitter from years ago, and my youth choir director from church when I was in middle school. I had spent twenty-five years of my life as an alcoholic, I led the league in blackouts and stupors, but this was a daze that left me completely dumbfounded. The look on my face must have been priceless as I was handed an apple plated in gold. Dr Gist, a huge smile across her face, said, "Mr. Shubert, we want to present you with the Golden Apple Award for Tulsa Public Schools and recognize you as one of our outstanding teachers." Two years prior to this, I was sitting in rehab, homeless, wondering why I even existed. Now, the fog was beginning to lift, my soul was beginning to see that purpose I had searched for, and it was the moment I got my first real taste of my secret sauce. And I am so thankful my wife had me change my shirt.

*I had no clue I was making a difference.
(Dr. Deborah Gist, Ron Terrell of Fox News, and me)*

I had no idea this was coming. If it weren't for the actions and words of one of my seventh-grade students, Frances, I would never have known the difference I was making as a teacher and a mentor. There was a great connection between the two of us. We talked about her mom fighting cancer and me not being able to see my daughter, Kamdyn. We lifted one another up. Little did I know that I had inspired her to be a teacher like me. She stood across from me as the reporter from Fox News handed me the Golden Apple. Dr. Gist began to read the letter Frances had written on my behalf. I felt humbled and was caught up in a rush of the greatest sense of purpose I had ever felt. Frances was the catalyst in opening my eyes to why I taught in the first place. Even more importantly, she changed my life in a way that I had hoped for but could never quite put meaning to.

Thanks to Frances, for the very first time I felt alive and that my life mattered. I was alive to give away what recovery from alcohol had given to me. I was the greatest miracle in the world, the only one of one hundred and seventeen billion people that had been or ever were on this planet that was just like me. Now I knew that I was to spend each day loving people and leading them to believe and discover that very same thing. I had searched for the vein of my existence for 46 years of my life, and a thirteen-year-old girl opened the door for me to find it. Frances, I do not know if you will ever read this, but I am going to send you the very first copy of this book. You may never know exactly what you did for me that day. It was mind-blowing to receive such an honor from the Tulsa Public School District; however, the game changer was realizing my ability to connect and build relationships with students that made a lifelong difference for them. Frances, you are the greatest miracle in the world. It was you who delivered me the key to unlocking the mystery in why my life mattered, why I was even here.

The Golden Apple still sits on my desk in my classroom as a reminder that my life is not all about me. Life is about excavating that treasure inside of us. Digging deep into our souls, our pasts, our wins, and our losses.

Being brave enough to step outside of our comfort zone, to take big risks, and to see past the fear of failure and success. Once we find that treasure, we become empowered by our natural gifts and abilities to impact people's lives. We realize that it was never about what we do in life or how we do it but why we do what we do. Realizing I had a purpose saved me from a death by alcoholism and awoke in my innermost being what I did best: connect with young people. Being an educator and a coach is what I do. The day I was handed that Golden Apple, one thing became crystal clear. Using my gifts coupled with sharing my story – the good, the bad, and the ugly – to build relationships became my superpower. It is yours too. It is our secret sauce.

CHAPTER TWO
Try harder, Daddy.

As a kid, I acquired some deep daddy issues. The divorce my parents went through was devastating to me. I got caught in the middle of it in ways I won't go into because it would not be fair to either of my parents. But there are things a twelve-year-old boy should not see or be brought into in an adult relationship. These issues would alter who I believed I was and erode all semblance of self-esteem I had. It was a dark time that became the catalyst for how I would perceive relationships as an adult and the scapegoat I would use to blame all my future failures upon. It was the beginning of me thinking my whole life was entirely about me.

Sharing our secret sauce is fueled by two things: Purpose and Relationships. However, until we learn why we have this secret sauce within us, it will never become the powerful force we need as educators. A vital lesson is necessary to understand and embrace the secret sauce within us all. It is the lesson of humility, which I would learn in the most painful way. Life will humble us, bring us down to our right size. I am grateful that I accepted the fact that I needed an apron of humility. Without it, I would never have been able to begin discovering and serving up that secret sauce.

As a young man, I did not possess the ability to understand purpose, and the relationships that I tried to build were almost always entirely unhealthy. In time, they would become toxic as I sucked the life out of each person I was connected to. I needed them to be the self-love that I could not give myself. I needed their constant validation that I was worthy of love. There was no intent to stand on my own; I needed a relationship to prop me up. I would smother the flame of each romantic relationship, then blame them for me looking elsewhere for someone new. I had vowed to not repeat some of my father's mistakes. A divorce, a broken home, was something I told myself I would never put on my kids, and I meant it. I just had no idea how to not let that happen. My soul was broken, and I was unaware that a relationship would never mend my crumbling heart. What I swore I would never do, I did. My life was all about me, and I would leave people devastated in my wake for many years to come. The ones I wanted to love and protect the most, my kids, are the very ones I crushed. Just like my dad had done to me.

I did not set out to hurt my kids, just as I am one hundred percent positive my dad did not set out to hurt me. But in 1990, the story began that would end up leaving my two boys crushed.

I was attending college at Oklahoma Christian University in Oklahoma City, OK. Education was secondary; I was there to play soccer, and I did it well. I gained a ton of recognition as an athlete, received award after award and, in spite of myself, was getting an education as well. My high school girlfriend followed me to college, and in June of 1990 we were going to get married. She was my crutch, my place to hide from the battle that raged within me: the war between who I knew I was at the time and who I really wanted to be. She was the sweetest girl but not anything I needed, and to be honest, I was the last thing she needed. Young and dumb, we got married, and she quickly became pregnant with my first son, Blake.

My senior year, we moved into an off-campus apartment while I tried to play athlete, student, best friend to my mates, father-to-be, and husband – in that order. I wanted the best of both worlds: single college athlete, chasing the party at every chance, with the escape to come home to a wife and baby on the way that gave me some sense of purpose. I will never forget the morning of April 23, 1991, when my wife's water broke, and we rushed to the hospital. I think I took off to the car without her or her bag. Another glimpse of my life being all about me. However, that day was one of the best days of my life. Seeing my son, Blake, being born was truly the most miraculous thing I had ever seen. I felt like Tom Hanks in *Castaway*, but instead of screaming, "I made fire," I held my son and was in awe that we had made this real, live baby boy. I was instantly connected. Unfortunately, I would end up needing him to feel like I was somebody. I missed the point that it wasn't about me any longer. It wasn't about my needs; it was about him. And he just needed his daddy.

Fourteen months later, our son, Brady, was born. My brother, Kerry, and I were eighteen months apart, and I wanted my kids to be that close too. Brady wanted to appear into this world the same morning I had opening tryouts for our first year soccer club. I had spent the entire spring recruiting as my brother and I would venture into the arena not just as players but coaches. I hustled my pregnant wife in labor into the car and headed for the soccer fields. The tryouts had to get started, and I was the one families were coming to see, to meet, and to play for. As I hopped out to get tryouts started, I told my wife to just honk the horn when it was time, and we would head to the hospital. It wasn't long before I heard that honk. I had gotten tryouts started, things were going well, I was going to be a success, and oh yeah, I was having another baby boy. Another one of the greatest days of my life, yet the focus was more on me than it was on anyone else, much less my wife and unborn son. When Brady was born, it was magnificent and scary. The umbilical cord was wrapped around his neck, and he was blue. I was paralyzed with fear, but as is his nature, he found a way. He began to cry, his color returned, and I knew this kid was going to be a warrior. What a day! A new soccer club was started, my second son was brought into the world, and all I could think about was me. I was so selfishly lost. Everything was for me, I was owed that, I needed it. Without it, I was just a broken soul and a failure. What I had thought would be my happily ever after, turned out to be the exact nightmare that I swore I would never let happen to my family or my children.

For a while, life seemed normal or what I thought normal was supposed to be like. I had a loving wife, two healthy kids, and a job as a teacher and a coach. My life seemed like the perfect picture of Americana on the outside. But inside, I was restless. My spirit was full of discontent, and I felt guilty because I knew I shouldn't be having those feelings. What was missing? Was it more value and recognition at work? Could it be that I needed to win more state championships as a coach? Was my marriage lacking in authentic love and commitment? All I knew was that Kip needed more. And I began to seek that more by chasing the party. Consequently, my boys would pay the ultimate price for my inability to develop a true relationship with myself. What I didn't realize was that all I needed was right there within me the whole time. I needed to love and be content with who I was and what

I had. In time, I would learn that no thing, no accomplishment, no other person could do that for me.

*I was failing as a father.
(Blake, Josie and Brady)*

My sons mean the world to me, but by the time they were eight and seven, I was focused more on my restlessness than on them. A couple nights a week, and maybe one on the weekend, I would get home from work and soccer practice, then eat, shower, and leave to go out with friends. It would be the beginning of a pattern that would lead me to my rock bottom. I chased the party, drank to get drunk, with the delusion that somehow I would meet someone that would take away the cloud of self-imposed depression that never would go away. It never really dawned on me on how it was affecting my children. They were going to bed right after I left. They were just little kids; they would be fine because I loved them and that was that. By not loving myself, I was failing as a father. I never developed the capacity to create the space for them that they needed because I had never created it for myself. My life was all about me. The cracks in the relationship between my wife and me widened into a canyon that was impossible to cross. In the year 2000, it would lead us to separate and eventually divorce.

At Thanksgiving of that year, she went to her parents' house, and I stayed at home. I remember being so heartbroken and hopeful all at the same time. My turkey dinner that year consisted of a case of beer, a bag of weed, chips, and nacho cheese dip. I spent the day feeling sorry for myself knowing that when my family returned we would tell the boys that their daddy was ripping their family apart and their hearts right out of their chests. The more I drank, the sadder and heavier my heart became. I escaped into the booze and the weed until I passed out. When I came to the next morning, there it was. That guilt, the selfish sadness, staring me right in the face. The alcoholic was born in that family room, and I didn't even know it. I would spend the next fourteen years running from facing the fact that I hated who I had become by escaping into as many cans of beer as I could stomach. Soon, I would hear the words from my youngest son that haunt me to this very day.

My wife and I agreed to tell the boys about the divorce after I returned from a weekend of partying and indoor soccer. When I walked in the door that Sunday evening, I dreaded what was about to happen, yet I had no intention of doing anything differently. The instant I hit the entryway I could sense the heartbreak. Something had already happened. My wife had decided to go ahead and tell the boys of our divorce. I was so angry, but she didn't know if I was going to show up, and she had a point. So, she just did it. She simply said, "They are in their room." I made my way down the L-shaped hallway to their bedroom. I had no idea what I was going to say, but it hit me that I had become exactly the man I had promised myself I would never become. I was about to do to my sons what my father had done to me.

As I entered the room, the look on their faces broke my heart. I immediately pushed that hurt deep down in my gut to avoid feeling the immense pain I could see in their eyes. I knew that life-altering pain, and here I was dishing it out on my boys. I said the words *it will be alright, we will always love you,* and *we will always take care of you.* None of it was any solace to them, and I knew it. They just wanted to know why. I didn't have the guts to tell them that their dad was unhappy and needed something more. I couldn't tell them their dad was broken and had no idea how to fix himself. I tried to comfort them as best as I could. I got to the point that I just couldn't stand the guilt of their tears washing over me. As I got up to leave their room, Brady, my youngest, grabbed my leg and started sobbing uncontrollably. The words he spoke reduce me to tears even as I write this. He simply cried out, "Try harder, Daddy. Try harder." What man would not at least give it one more go after a request like that? ME. I looked at him with tears in my eyes and said, "I did, Son," and I walked out of the room.

I hated myself. To this day, I am disgusted by what I did to my boys. It was the teeth of a lesson I would learn sitting in rehab fourteen years later. Hurt people hurt people, which is true, but to me, it was an excuse. The fact was, my life was all about me. I sought meaning and purpose in others. I destroyed people in my selfish pursuits for the promised land. I learned the hard way that the life we dream of doesn't find us in what we get or who we have. The life we dream of finds us when we live to give to others, taking our talents, our abilities, our stories and giving them away freely. When I learned to love myself, I could do that. The life I sought was right inside me all along. I am just sorry I had to hurt so many, especially the ones I loved the most, to find it. I hear Brady's words each day in my head, "Try harder, Daddy," and I do. My life today is not all about me. Learning the lesson of humility was the first step to my eyes being opened to the wonder in us all. It was the first step in me finding that secret sauce.

CHAPTER THREE
Rock Bottom to Recovery

Sometimes, life's most painful, humbling experiences can become the most defining moments we ever live through. Hitting rock bottom proved to be the teacher of the lesson I had to learn to discover that I possessed a secret sauce. A gift within me that was meant to impact the lives of others, not just my own. Landing in a rehab facility on March, 21, 2014 was the day the lesson really began, and as painful and heart breaking as it was then, I am forever grateful that rock bottom found me. I was running from it as fast as I could drink, and without the lesson that was so needed, I would have been dead within months.

Almost everyone remembers the lyrics, "Going to the chapel..." from the old song *Chapel of Love* by The Dixie Cups. Going to the chapel was where I found recovery. In that tiny space of heaven, on the front pew, is where I finally learned that life was not all about me.

Rock bottom was a long time coming. By the time I was 46, I had spent twenty five years of my life chasing the party. Weekends, holidays, tailgates, you name it, any excuse to have a good time. Every single time, I drank to get drunk. I did not understand moderation, I only knew to go big or go home. What started as one or two days a week, had grown to six or seven days a week. By the end, I was drinking until I blacked out, going big and never knowing how the hell I got home. Two divorces, big wins and big failures as a teacher and coach, and the haunting fact that I had totally blown it as a father all led to me spiral out of control. I was in flames and heading for a crash that would kill a part of me that needed to die. Fortunately, that would give life to a part of me that desperately wanted to live. By March of 2014, I was a full-blown alcoholic. I wanted to try harder; I wanted to be the man I knew was in that black hole inside my soul. But life was about me, why wouldn't people just love me, save me, fix me? I had no idea I would find my answer in the best teacher I have ever had: rock bottom.

On March 21, 2014, I said goodbye to my family and friends. The last phone conversation I had before leaving was with my oldest son, Blake. His words were simple, I just want my dad back. I was headed to a thirty day vacation. Free food, a warm place to sleep, and these people were going to teach me how to drink like a gentleman. I still had no idea I was an alcoholic, no sense of reality of the damage I had done and was still doing to my children; it was still all about Kip. I was going to become the respectable life of the party, not just the drunk who had to be carried home. *Try harder, Daddy; I just want my dad back*, were not just words but pleas of desperation that would have gotten most fathers' attention. But not mine. I heard them, but I did not *hear* them. The noise from the pity party I was drowning in canceled out their cries. I had lost my car. I had lost my home. For crying out loud, I was homeless! My teaching job was hanging on by a fraying thread called FMLA. All I needed was a major reset at the Valley Hope resort for addicts and alcoholics. I mean what else could go wrong, right? I was about to find out just how rocky the bottom would become.

My little one, Kamdyn, and me.

I had lost almost everything. One of the few things I had left was my five-year-old daughter, Kamdyn. To this day I call her my saving grace, and I know she has little understanding of the weight that title holds. I could not lose Kamdyn, she was the last glimmer of hopeful light left in an ever growing world of darkness. But I still had not learned the lesson my boys had tried to teach me, *try harder, Daddy.*

The Christmas before I went into rehab I had Kamdyn from the day her school was out through Christmas Eve, it would be her mother's turn to have her on Christmas Day. I was drinking constantly and in a horrible place mentally. All I could think about was being at the bar. Somehow, that would make it better, and that elusive savior I had been seeking would appear. On the night before Christmas Eve, I called my boys to come over to babysit. I used them often to cover for me while I spent time at the bars until well into the early morning.

Kamdyn and I spent the day Christmas shopping. I was hungover and was counting the minutes, the seconds, until I could find my way back to my favorite watering hole. My boys arrived, and I spent a few minutes getting ready to leave. As I came into the living room, I began to tell Kamdyn that I had to go out, but I would be back soon. I picked her up to kiss her goodbye, and she embraced me with a death grip. Crying, she said the words that not only cut me deep, but I am sure brought back such painful emotions for my boys. She sobbed,

"Daddy, please don't go. Don't go, Daddy." Again, I left anyway. I could feel the pull of the good guy inside telling me to stay, but the power of addiction makes a man do things he swears he would never do.

The next morning, we celebrated Christmas. It wasn't as jovial as you might imagine. I am sure my boys were put out with me leaving yet again, and Kamdyn, I am sure, was heartbroken. There were a few smiles as we opened gifts, and I fought off a hangover. Those were getting easier and easier to overcome as the alcohol took over, not just my mind but my body as well. Honestly, all I could think about or even cared about was how many hours it would be until they were gone so I could begin the day's drunken cycle all over again. By early in the afternoon all of my children had left. They would never come back to that home again. I would only see Kamdyn one more time before I went into rehab that coming March. The addiction was too strong at that point, and I was in such bad shape I made excuses not to have her on my weekends. I could not go a day without drinking, and I knew I could not let her see me in that condition. Since all I could think about was me, in my mind, I was doing her a favor. From that Christmas to March, I would lose my house, my car, and any self-respect I had left. On March 21, 2014, I was headed to Valley Hope in Cushing, Oklahoma in my brother's car. My 30-day vacation was about to begin, I would learn to party, drink, and do it all responsibly. What else did I have to lose? I mean, what else could go wrong? I was at rock bottom, right? I had no idea the greatest loss, the real rock bottom, was coming for me, and it would be the wake-up call that saved my life.

I was about to be taught the greatest lesson of my life. A week into my stay in rehab, a voice came across the facility's loudspeaker, "Kip Shubert, please report to your counselor's office." My first thought was that I had been doing so well I was going to be sent home with a certificate that I was not a drunk anymore. When I got to her door, I knocked, and she asked me to come in and have a seat. The look on her face was not one of celebration. As I sat down she looked at me and said, "I have some news I need to share with you." Did someone die, I thought? In a sense, I was about to. In the most loving, gentle way she began to explain to me that through the courts my ex-wife had been granted sole custody of Kamdyn. But it was worse than that. All of my parental rights had been stripped away, and I was forbidden to contact, communicate, or even see my little girl again. That was the news that finally broke my selfish, stubborn, alcoholic spirit. My angel, the little ray of sunshine that shone in my life, was gone. I sat there and sobbed one of those ugly cries, just like I had the night my dad left when I was thirteen. Rock bottom had found me; it was a hurt I had never experienced. It felt like my heart had literally been broken into a million pieces. Now, I had nothing left, no purpose, no reason to live. My counselor hugged me, and I walked down the hallway back to my room. I was going to pack my things, leave, and drink myself to death. But the chapel I would pass on the way had other ideas.

As I passed the chapel doors, something stopped me. I believe it was God who was calling me back home like the prodigal son. I opened the door, walked to the front of the chapel and plopped down on the first pew. I looked up at the crucifix that was on the wall, and that ugly cry came flooding back. All I could think was WHY ME?! How did I get here? What had gone so wrong in my life that I was at the point of wanting to die? It was over; I was out of chances. I had earned the title of the biggest loser. As I stared up at that wall, wishing Jesus would appear and take me, I uttered one word. It was just a word, but the power of it saved my life. The one word that changed everything was simply *help*.

HELP

I meant it with every ounce of sincerity left in my body. I was out of options. I had screwed up so badly I could never fix it on my own. For the first time, life wasn't all about me. I said the word help not for me but for Kamdyn. She was my saving grace at that horrific rock bottom. My mind shifted from thinking about myself and why me, to thinking about her. She needed her dad. I still had life left in me, and with what little was there, I uttered that one word. Instantly, it felt like someone from behind reached under my arms and lifted me to a standing position. I felt a warmth that pulsed throughout my entire body. My tears dried up, and I could sense a courage inside me that I thought had been lost many years ago. My spirit saw a glimmer of hope. I could smell love in the air around me, like the sweet aroma from a spring flower garden. I suddenly began to feel alive. I have no doubt that it was God. He had never left me, no matter how far I had tried to run from Him. Addiction is a deadly disease that isn't cured in a moment. It takes daily work to heal and overcome, but in that moment, I could hear God whisper in my ear,

"You are the greatest miracle in the world, and we have work to do."

I listened, and I believed Him. I have not drunk a drop of alcohol since that night. The most defining moment in my life happened in that chapel; I realized there was so much more to life than just Kip. I had work to do. I had to recover, not for me but for others. One day at a time, I would begin to discover that I had a secret sauce.

What I have come to realize is that we all have a secret sauce. Most of us either don't believe it or are so wrapped up in ourselves that we never find it. Our *why me* moments need to become *why not me*. Every single one of us has experiences – good, bad, and ugly – that make up our story. As educators, we have tremendous gifts and abilities. Stir all these ingredients together, and you have your secret sauce, which develops those life-changing relationships that are the backbone of why we do what we do. I would not wish rock bottom on anyone, but that is what it took for me to figure out the real meaning of why I am here. What will it take for *you* to find the real meaning of why you are here? What will it take for all of us in education to see it is not about us? We have the most powerful, most wonderful, and most underrated job in the world. We get to love others and lead them to believe and discover that they are the greatest miracle in the world. God whispered this to me, and I am shouting it to you and anyone else who will listen. There is a secret sauce we all have within us, and I am going to share the ingredients with you. The ingredients will not only change the way you teach, the way you coach, and the way you lead but will change your relationships. And the sauce will change your life.

CHAPTER FOUR
A Giant Stuffed Animal

The secret sauce is full of different ingredients. Every person has their own unique blend that creates an individual flavor to bring your ability to teach, coach, and relate to others to the next level. We have established that, as educators, we need to learn the necessary lesson of humility if we really want to reach into the hearts of our young people and pull out all of the greatness and unlimited potential in them. However, we all must start with one ingredient that is the base to becoming an educator who is a game changer for their kids, their school, and their communities. Self-love, believing that we are worthy, will allow us to grasp and use that secret sauce to change lives. Let's be honest. How can we ever love others and lead them to believe and discover that they are the greatest miracle in the world if we first do not believe that about ourselves?

For me, the lack of self-love and belief in myself led me to think that my life was all about me. It caused insecurity and self-doubt within me. I needed people and things to fill that void. Surely, if I had the prettiest wife, the best group of friends, and achieved all the greatest rewards that would equal the self-love I didn't even know I was lacking. It never did though. That gaping hole in my heart would fill for an instant, but it was a mirage. In fact, these things didn't really even fill that hole. Those substitutes for self-love just made the hole bigger. Eventually, that severe drought of belief that I was worthy of a life worth living, that I was even good enough to become that somebody I had dreamed of as a child, led me to an addiction to alcohol. I drowned myself in booze to escape the fact that my life, my soul, and my heart were empty, loveless. If I was going to know love, find that secret sauce, self-love was a lesson I had to learn. That lesson came in the most unforeseen and unbelievable way. It was an oversized, stuffed dog that would do the teaching. Strange, right? Just wait; it gets better.

After my chapel moment, it finally hit me that the universe did not revolve around Kip. When my flaws and failures suddenly became a source of strength to rebuild my life instead of the excuses to blame everyone else for my downfall, I was presented with the tools to discover self-love for the very first time. My counselor, Christie, was overjoyed that I decided to stay and embrace the healing process of recovery. As I sat in her office for one of our weekly sessions, she described how we must first love who we are right now. We must meet ourselves where we are, much like we need to do for our students and staff. We discussed self-affirmations and their importance. She outlined things I could do to begin acquiring the much needed ability to love who I was right then and who I could become. Then, she began to explain an exercise she wanted me to do for the next week. As the words came out of her mouth, I thought what she was proposing sounded crazy. I was to carry this three-foot, stuffed dog around with me everywhere. I was to take care of it for one week. I could never leave it unattended, and I could not allow anyone to take control of its whereabouts for me. It was up to me; it needed me. Without me, it could not make it through the week. How was this inconvenient and embarrassing task supposed to help me find the self-love and self-worth that had escaped me since the divorce of my parents when I was 12? It sounded like all it would do was make me look like a jackass.

I reluctantly took that big dog under my arm and headed out her door to a week that was sure to be full of embarrassment and teasing. I carried him to my room and sat there wondering if this thing called recovery was real or just some racket to fleece the families of addicts and alcoholics. However, I remembered the words *try harder, Daddy*, and I could see the confusion and hurt on Kam's face in my mind, wondering where her daddy had gone. It was all the motivation I needed to suck it up and push through the week. After everything I had experienced in that chapel, how bad could it be to carry around a giant stuffed animal?

The first couple of days were not really that bad. I had this strange sense of urgency to make sure that dog was safe at all times. I did not let go of it very often, and I dared not let it out of my sight. Rehab is notorious for crazy pranksters, and I could only imagine what someone might do to him all in the name of fun. In our downtime at rehab, we could smoke cigarettes, drink coffee, or goof off with other residents. Goofing off became what we did with what little free time we had; we looked forward to it. So, I knew that my giant stuffed dog would not be safe around my buddies if I did not get serious about taking care of him. Coupled with carrying this dog around were morning and evening self-affirmations. In the morning, I was to hold my dog, and in front of the bathroom mirror, read self-affirmations aloud. I felt like Stuart Smalley from *Saturday Night Live*, saying to myself as I held that puppy, I am good enough, I am smart enough, and doggonit people like me. Before bed, I was required to read these affirmations again but to my roommate. My roommate, Aaron, who I still consider a dear friend to this day, listened and played along. One evening, we were both in bed, but I had forgotten to read my affirmations. I coaxed Aaron out of bed, and there we sat, two grown men in their underwear, one reading self-affirmations like Stuart Smalley, the other listening. It would become a moment in time I will never forget. This guy I had known for just a week or two, cared enough about me to sit there in his underwear, while another grown man in his underwear read to him. I admit we began to laugh halfway through it. I could not keep a straight face. But that comedic moment of vulnerability would bond Aaron and me together in a way that could never be broken. Not only was I beginning to understand how to care for myself, I was finding out that others really cared about me. Aaron, wherever you are, I love you, buddy.

Later on that week, I got complacent with the dog a couple of times. I left it at my seat in a class to go up and ask a question, and when I came back, he was gone. I would later find him in the women's restroom. I also left him on the couch in the TV room to run to the bathroom. I was the only one there and was sure I would be quick. Less than a minute later, I came out of the bathroom, and again, he was gone. Ironically, I found him in the front row of that chapel. I felt a sense of panic each time I lost him. It was like a part of me was taken away, and I just had to find it. I was growing increasingly attached to that stuffed dog. I cared for him, and nothing was going to hurt him. I wasn't going to let him down. What I was learning was this oversized stuffed canine was becoming the very person I had never learned to care for, ME.

The week came to a close and I was called back into my counselor's office to discuss the experience. We laughed over the affirmations in the underwear and cried over the lesson that I was beginning to grasp. She shared with me that the foundation for my recovery began within me. For me to ever begin to truly believe in others, I had to believe in myself. Self-love became the foundation on which I rebuilt my life. It allowed me to put into practice that my life was about others, not just myself.

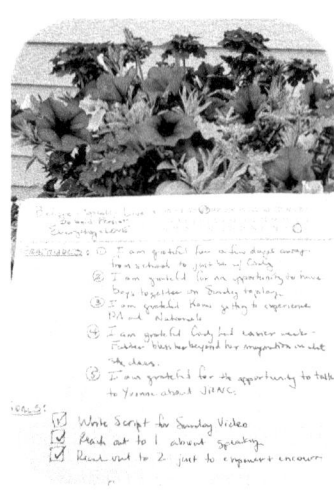

my journal

From that week on, I have worked daily on loving me exactly as I am today. I meet myself where I am. Affirmations are still read daily, I set goals for the day, and top it off with a serving of daily gratitudes I write in my journal. Knowing that I truly am the greatest miracle in the world allowed me to shed the guilt and shame from my past. It got me out of my own pity party and into the business of serving others with my why. As educators, we sometimes lose that along the way. The Covid era had a way of hiding our why from many of us.

But my recovery taught me such a valuable lesson in self-love. Loving myself gave me the tools to live out my purpose. I didn't need others to validate me anymore. Status, relationships, achievement were not a requirement for me to feel good about who I was becoming. I could finally put all that energy into that secret sauce I had been gifted. No longer is that secret sauce there to make me feel ok with being an alcoholic. It is to share with every student and athlete in front of me and anyone else in this world who needs it. I really was good enough, and I really was smart enough.

If we truly want to be that greatest miracle in the world in all we do, it starts with meeting ourselves where we are and loving who we are right now. If you need a giant stuffed animal to do it, then get one. Self-love unlocks the kitchen to begin cooking up that secret sauce to feed others, not just ourselves. Teaching is not about us as educators, and our secret sauce isn't either. We must believe in what we do and love ourselves as teachers, coaches and administrators. If we don't, how can we expect everyone else to believe in the greatest profession in the world and love those that dedicate their lives to it?

CHAPTER FIVE
It is what it is.

So, what do you do when you begin to learn to love yourself? What is the next step in discovering that secret sauce within you? I love myself, great, but what do I do with my past, my present, my future and the overload of anxiety that comes with it? After the experience with that giant stuffed dog, I began to feel like my head was above water for the first time in a long, long time. However, I was treading water, and to get to a place with some solid footing, it would take another ingredient for me to be able to recognize and begin to harness that power within my secret sauce. I have heard the saying, it is what it is, way too many times. Funny thing is, I use it a lot now. To me it always carried an air of hopelessness and resigning yourself to a bad hand you had been dealt. But the most important thing I learned in the various rooms of Alcoholics Anonymous meetings was the necessary partner to self-love: acceptance. On page 413 of my *Big Book*, I have it highlighted and underlined several times. Acceptance is the answer to all of my problems today. As a man in recovery, it is what it is wasn't a hopeless or contrite saying; it would be the ladder I would use to begin climbing back to a life of purpose. I found the answer to meeting myself exactly where I was. Acceptance was the key that unlocked my ability to finally see what I had lost back in my youth, that special something that all that I could not control had covered in darkness. Acceptance unveiled what I had felt in my soul but could never quite understand or grasp. I was worth it, I was good enough, just as I was. I stopped running from that inner gift that had always called my name. Now, I was able to run to it unafraid; I was no longer in need of hiding from that secret sauce.

Heading to the AA meetings at the beginning of my recovery was a humbling experience. I had become one of *those* people. People with a stigma that I have come to learn is unfair and, in many cases, untrue. Alcoholics and addicts are not what we see in the media, movies, or on our urban area streets. They are white collar, blue collar, and homeless. They are all colors, creeds, and races. Men, women, young and old. They are your neighbors and your co-workers. This deadly disease of addiction does not discriminate. I sat around and across tables from people who were much like me, and I learned to begin to accept who I had become. Yet, I also saw who I *could* become, and that would be a game changer for me. I never thought in a million years that I would end up in rehab, having to go to a meeting or two a day, homeless, no vehicle, and no parental rights to my child. However, there I was, in those rooms, everyday saying, "Hi, my name is Kip, and I am an alcoholic."

I learned a great deal about the 12 steps. They are actually a great set of principles to live your life by whether you have a problem with drugs and alcohol or not. There was also a ton of wisdom around me in those chairs. Men and women with decades of sobriety, with amazing stories of overcoming adversity that made my struggles seem not so bad. It became a routine that I needed to stay sober, or so I thought. Daily, I would check the box of going to a meeting, and that was supposed to be the antidote to my alcoholism. Each day, I would recite the same things, hear the same tales and advice, and it started to become mundane. What did it all mean? Did I have to attend a meeting every single day for the rest of my life? Was I trading the bar for the rooms of AA? Something was stirring in me, and for the life of me, I could not put a finger on it.

About a year into my recovery, some things began to click for me. The repetition of Alcoholics Anonymous meetings had seeped through my thick skull and into my brain. One day, sitting around the table, the saying *one day at a time* finally made sense. The thing that mattered most was that day, right then. It was the only day with that date that I would get. The present, being in the moment, was more important than the guilt and shame of my past and the worries of what would become of me in the future. It is a realization I still use each day, and it makes me a more effective teacher and coach. I can't change yesterday, and tomorrow will come when it comes, but I can choose to make a difference today. Being present has brought back that feeling of being alive. My energy is focused solely on doing the next right thing and taking in all today has to offer. My past taught me I don't want to miss another moment in the present. When I teach, when I coach, we have an endgame in mind. We have set goals, but we focus on the process. Taking care of each step, one day at a time, is our insurance that we will achieve the things we set out to do. It's the simple things that can teach us so much. You can know every pedagogical trick in the book, but if you can't stay present, can't be in the moment with your kids, one day at a time, then you are missing the boat.

The lesson those rooms taught me that made the biggest difference though was acceptance. "Acceptance is the answer to all of my problems today. When I find someone, something, or some situation unacceptable to me I can find no peace until I accept that it is what it is at that moment. I need to focus on what needs changed in me and not on what needs changed in the world around me," (AA World Services, 2009). I still write this saying out daily in my morning journal time, even now. I've said it so frequently at home that my wife cuts me off with an, "I know, I know," before I even finish. But there is so much truth in it. If I am feeling guilty, ashamed, or resentful about my past, I can't be present today. If I am stressed about tomorrow, the future, what we will do if…, then I can't be present today. It removes the anxiety that would leave me needing to get drunk seven days a week. It shifts my mindset to the right now, and that is always more manageable. I can live in the moments I used to miss. As an educator, I can focus on the kids that are right in front of me, and the lesson, the discussion, the practice, and the growth going on directly in front of my eyes. Last week's failed plans, next week's upcoming evaluation, don't take energy away from me connecting, building relationships, and loving and leading my students. Because life is what it is. Today is what it is, and I get to do all I can to make it better, to make an impact that just might keep a kid from going through the hell I experienced. Why? It's simple. One day at a time, I practice ACCEPTANCE.

In my first two years of recovery, I never missed a meeting. Many days, I would attend two. But I began to grow restless. I was living one day at a time. I had accepted life as it was, but I had this tremendous force in me whispering that there was more for me. That force was my secret sauce calling me to action. It had been sitting there inside me my whole life waiting to be discovered, disciplined, and shaped into the powerful gift it was meant to be. This time, I didn't start looking for someone to blame. The excuses that used to be so easily accessible to me were nowhere to be found. I didn't even feel the need to complain, I just felt compelled to move, to grow. Like a seed covered in dirt, I had been watered and fertilized, and I could feel the warmth of the sun coaxing me to make my presence known above ground. Purpose was pumping through my veins, and I had the most profound desire to find it.

One day, I sat in a meeting, and as I looked around the room, I saw faces that were devoid of that same purpose that was burning in me. I didn't want to be decades sober, telling the same story, once a day, just to be sober. I wanted to feel as alive as I could possibly feel so I walked out of that meeting knowing that I would not be back on any sort of consistent basis. I am grateful for the lessons the 12-step program of Alcoholics Anonymous instilled in me, but it was time to get into the arena and fight. One day at a time, I would focus on what needed to be better in me so I could be that educator, coach, and speaker I had always known I was destined to be. There would be a process of growth, ups and downs, losses and wins, and I was ready for them. If I did not get back into the game, dirty and bloody from the fight, I could not feel that sense of every cell in my body feeling totally full of the vigorous energy of life. And the key was so simple: acceptance. It is still the answer to all of my problems today. We are worth it, we are more than good enough, and when we tackle life one day at a time, we can not only dream big, we can live big. Sure, there will be challenges, maybe even great adversity, but there will also be great success and achievement. When we accept life on life's terms, no matter what comes our way today, we know we will thrive through it. Simply because it is what it is.

CHAPTER SIX
Getting My Daughter Back

The driving force behind me learning to stay clean and sober one day at a time was my little 6-year-old angel, Kamdyn Preslee. The knowledge of losing all my parental rights and the ability to see or contact her was the catalyst that drove me to rebound from rock bottom. That crash didn't crush me; it became the fuel of adversity that drove me to sobriety. All of a sudden life was no longer just about me, it was way bigger, it was about that little blonde-headed angel I call my saving grace. She deserved *her* dad, not just *a* dad. In that early part of my recovery, it was who and what I thought of every single day. When I felt like I wanted to quit, I could hear Brady saying, "Try harder, Daddy," and Kamdyn saying, "Daddy, please don't go." When life hands us adversity, I have learned that we do one of two things. We can run, but it eventually consumes us, or we stand

and use it as fuel to become better. Knowing our purpose allows us to stand in the face of that monster and not run. And when I didn't think I could stand any more, still, I stood because I remembered a saying introduced to me by Pastor Bill Scheer from Tulsa, OK. That phrase would carry me through the fight of getting my daughter back. I knew I had a purpose that was bigger than just me, and I had that phrase, "If you don't quit, you win."

Losing Kamdyn was one of the most difficult doses of adversity I have ever had to navigate. It has also become one of my biggest advantages. The lessons I learned through it have proven invaluable to my secret sauce. It was an ingredient that I had never had in my life before. This lesson would make me a warrior in the classroom and on the soccer field, but it also made me into the man I had desired to be for such a long time. I knew I could connect, I had an innate ability to relate to young people. It was my destiny to be in front of them, loving and leading them. But I had always lacked one key trait, perseverance. Before going through this, I usually quit when the going got too tough. Again, I do not think the fear of failing troubled me; it was the fear of succeeding. I would self-sabotage anything good in my life, personally or professionally, to protect myself from being unable to sustain things of real value. The lack of self-love prevented me from believing I was good enough or worthy enough, to be a real success. I hid in the mediocrity of my teaching and coaching while, at the same time, becoming resentful for not being able to achieve what I knew in my soul I was destined to achieve. I just didn't have the intestinal fortitude to get to that next level. Having my daughter ripped out of my life enabled me to add perseverance to my secret sauce. I just had no idea how long and brutal this lesson was going to be.

How hard could it be? I was in recovery; I had a couple of months of sober time. Of course, I was stable enough to be back in my daughter's life. I would quickly learn that not everyone, actually most of the people we affect with our addictions, believes in our newfound life of sobriety. In the case of custody of my daughter, her mother would have no interest in believing in my sobriety, nor would she care how well I became. What I thought would be an easy fix, would become one hundred times the opposite. I figured that when I contacted my ex-wife and she knew that I was better, all would be forgotten. Things would go back to normal with our divorce decree and visitation schedule. To this day, I don't think she ever really cared if Kamdyn saw me, had her dad in her life. Either way, that isn't the point. I don't, and never did, control my ex-wife's actions or the actions of others. The fact is, Kamdyn did need me and still does. I finally knew that, and I would finally learn to advocate for myself and fight for others, no matter what it would take. There was no legal, health-related, or other reason for it to take as long as it did or be as hard as it was. Yet, I am so grateful that it did because it was the lesson I needed to become the man, the husband, the father, the teacher, and the coach I was created to be.

For the first year of my sobriety, I would call, text, and even write letters to my ex-wife telling her how good I was doing and that there were no reasons for concern on her part in me seeing my daughter again. I usually got no response, but when I did it was usually a good cussing ending with, "You will never see her again." It had begun to weigh on me. The frustration and resentment were beginning to boil over, and I was coming face to face with the hardest thing I have ever had to grow through. My usual behavior was to turn and run from the conflict, to drink and make excuses, but this time was different. I could stand in the face of adversity. The lesson of perseverance was being taught, and I didn't even realize it.

I had no true sober friends. My older boys were close by in Oklahoma City but were still keeping me at arm's length. I did not hold that against them in the least, but I needed support; I needed family. So, I decided to quit my teaching job in Yukon, OK and move back to Tulsa. My mom was there, two of my siblings, and many high school friends who supported me. It would also be where I would meet my wife, Cindy. I was learning that I had to take care of myself if I wanted to be the father my children needed. Thanks to that big, stuffed dog, I was advocating for me so I could get my kids back into my life. It would prove to be a great move. The lesson was about to get much harder, and I would need the emotional support and encouragement of my family.

A lot would happen in the next two years. I would finally develop a romantic relationship that was real, authentic, and lasting. God sent an angel my way, a woman who would become not just my wife but my best friend. We had both hit some hard times, and as time proved, were just what the other needed. I had a successful teaching career again in the Tulsa Public School system. My older kids were coming around and could see that their dad truly was a different man. Life seemed to be coming together, except there was one huge hole still in my heart, Kamdyn. There was not a day that went by when I didn't wonder where she was, what she was doing, what she looked like. I would get the occasional picture from her older sister. My mom and my sister were allowed to visit a few times and would report back to me on how she was doing. But the more healthy I became, the less that was allowed to happen. I was having ugly cries on the regular, it was ripping my heart apart not being allowed to be in her life. I could not figure out what else I needed to do to convince her mother otherwise. Going the legal route with an experienced, quality attorney was an option, but it would take me several years to save for the $10,000 retainer that would be required to take my case. I was doing better one day at a time, yet with Kamdyn, I was getting nowhere. I remember walking the neighborhood one morning and talking to God. I finally said, "Father, enough is enough. Kamdyn needs her daddy. I have fought, I have never given up, and will continue as long as it takes, but God – enough is enough."

Cindy and I began to put a plan together on how to afford the legal battle that was looming before us. It would be a real fight since the judge in the county was the former boss and best friend of my ex-wife's attorney. We had the best lawyer we could find and it was not going to be cheap. We took the two hour drive to Norman, OK to meet with her. She would require $5,000 upfront and another $5,000 to round out the retainer fee, plus all the other hours and court costs that were to follow. On a teacher's salary, I had no idea how we were going to afford it, but we were going to make it happen. It was quite intimidating sitting in front of her large executive desk. But as she listened to my story I could see that she would be in my corner. We finished the free consultation and headed back to Tulsa to finalize payment and our decision on how to proceed. I met with our pastor at our church and prayed for an outcome that would reunite Kam and me. I didn't know how this was all going to work or how long it would take in the court system, but I had faith that it would all work out. Faith was something I never had much of in my life previously, but this time I would see the miracle up close and personal.

*The little blonde headed angel
I call my saving grace*

The very next day my phone rang; it was my ex-wife. Let me preface this with the fact that she had no idea we were about to take her back into a legal battle. Her first words were, "Would you like to see your daughter"? I was shocked! Excuse me, could you repeat that? I could not believe what I was hearing, but it was that simple. We set a time for the coming weekend for me to come to Oklahoma City, meet with her and pick up Kamdyn. On the way there that Saturday, I had a flat tire. I changed it faster than Jeff Gordon's pit crew. Nothing was going to deter me from getting my daughter. I met with her mother and let her say everything she needed to, then agreed to her conditions. It wasn't about me, or even how unfair things had been, it was only about seeing Kam. Funny thing was, my ex-wife was dating someone who was also in recovery, and he was a main player in making this meeting happen. Kamdyn ran and jumped into my arms when she saw me. My fears that she had forgotten her daddy were quickly debunked. From that day forward, Kamdyn has been back in my life. It hasn't always been easy, and we have had to maneuver through many emotions together. Nevertheless, we are together. Just when I thought I was at the end of my rope, when enough was enough, God gave me a miracle. He brought back that little blonde-headed angel I call my saving grace.

The lesson on perseverance had been taught, and I had passed. It developed a grit in me that I now use in building relationships with students and improving cultures in schools. I do not know how to quit anymore. Perseverance wasn't just for me either. I am now able to believe in others unconditionally. I cannot quit them. If I say, "I will never let go, Jack," then I won't. Sorry, I wasn't there for you on the Titanic. My belief, my faith, was developed with such a strength that in my classrooms and locker rooms, my students can rent my belief until they can find their own. I used to quit when I knew greatness was right around the corner. Now, I run to it; I embrace it. I relish the challenge in getting there. I couldn't drink again if I wanted to. It serves no purpose because I found my why: to love kids and lead them to believe and discover that they are the greatest miracle in the world. It took me three years to get back into Kamdyn's life. It was the most painful and difficult journey through adversity I have ever been on. But it had to happen that way. I had to learn to persevere. I had to be shown that the secret sauce is a weapon of a warrior. And I learned, perseverance is the ingredient of our secret sauce that allows us to go into battle day after day, with faith and a promise that we matter, that we make a difference. Enough was enough, and a miracle happened in my life that brought my daughter and me back together. With perseverance added to our secret sauce, we become the educators our kids desperately need because we know one truth: when you don't quit, you win.

CHAPTER SEVEN
A Warrior's Mindset

Getting my daughter back into my life was probably the happiest moment of my life. It felt like I had not just climbed Mount Everest but whipped its tail. I was on top of the world, overjoyed! Life was becoming more normal a day at a time, and I was relishing in the success that was flooding into my life. But you know, life is really funny. I tell my classes and teams this all the time because I have learned from experience that life never stops throwing sucker punches. They keep coming, one after the other, your whole life. It's not if and when you get hit with adversity; it is how you respond to it and develop the ability to get back up each time life knocks you down. I believe that God was preparing me for what was to come with the experience of three years of perseverance in fighting to see my daughter again. I needed to learn the value of the warrior's mindset. I had to practice, day in and day out, that when I did not quit, I would win. I really believe that. Because what was headed our way would take every ounce of strength I had learned in my recovery.

My kids were coming around, my little one was back, and on top of that, I was in the very first real, authentic, romantic relationship in my life. The moment I didn't need another woman to complete me was the moment I could begin to entertain finding one again. And not just any woman, but the woman who was perfect for me. Cindy was unlike any other woman I had been in a relationship with before. Previously, all I ever wanted was the opposite of what I really needed, but she was exactly what I needed now: an encourager, an unconditional ally, a best friend, and someone that would not put up with any bull. She held me accountable, she made me want to be a better man every day and not just for her, but for everyone who I would impact in my life. I had never experienced that type of connection before. And, although it isn't always flawless, it is imperfectly perfect for us. I never refer to her, or even think of her, as my third wife, she is just my wife, *the* wife. She has been by my side through it all, helping me get to things and places I had never reached or seen before. She has my back. Now, it was time for me to have hers.

Cindy is meticulous in all she does. She takes her time, dots all the i's, and crosses all the t's. Perfect for me since I live in a way that can only be called the opposite. Even when it comes to her health. She is the woman that schedules all the necessary appointments and has her yearly check-up. I have to have a body part falling off to go see a doctor. In the summer of 2017, we were planning to leave on our week-long annual vacation. We were headed to the Smoky Mountains, a first for both of us. But before we left Cindy had her yearly check-up. There were no concerns other than the fact that she had been more tired than normal recently. She received her usual clean bill of health except for one hiccup. On her blood panels, her overall proteins were considerably high. The doctor didn't seem concerned and attributed it to a possible diet anomaly. He just told her to enjoy the vacation, eat a little better and come in next month to redo her blood work. This seemed easy enough, not even enough to really raise an alarm for either of us. We headed to the Smokies and had the best week. It was just us, and we enjoyed being in a beautiful place together. I had accepted a new job in Sapulpa, OK. I was back in the coaching game again. My daughter was back. I had the most amazing wife. Adversity? No way; I had overcome all that. At least, I thought I had.

After our vacation, life kept cruising right along. I began the process of rebuilding the boy's soccer program at Sapulpa High School, and Cindy and I were thriving. Kamdyn was a regular visitor every other weekend, and life was just so much better than it had been three to four years before. When it came to the end of the month Cindy had her appointment for the re-screening of her blood panel. We expected everything to be fine, but it would turn out to be the opposite. Her total protein levels were higher. So, the doctor gave her a number to call, saying he was making a referral and that she needed to set up an appointment. When Cindy made that call her life changed in an instant. As it rang, she waited for the answer on the other end of the line, thinking nothing serious. But when they answered, it was the last thing she was expecting. On the other end a voice said, "Thank you for calling St. Francis Oncology, how can I help you?" Her heart must have sunk to the bottom of her feet. Kind of a cruel twist, but the doctor didn't tell her who he was referring her to, so she was left wondering if she had some sort of cancer. An appointment was hastily scheduled for the next week, and Cindy began to research day and night. What the heck could be wrong with her? She had only felt more tired than usual; surely, it was nothing. We both felt the gravity of the situation, and I would not let her attend the appointment alone.

At the appointment, we met her new cancer specialist, Dr. Kalim. His bedside manner was amazing and helped us feel as calm and secure as we possibly could. They did a ton of blood work, so much that I could not watch. Needles make me pass out. Then, they took a marrow biopsy out of her back. It was like watching the doctor put a corkscrew into her. I have never seen such strength with a smile during a procedure that I knew had to be excruciatingly painful. And Cindy just kept smiling. I was beginning to see the next lesson on the list of ingredients to that secret sauce. She had prepared herself with the mindset of a warrior. She *believed* she was going to be ok, she *said* that she was going to be ok, and she would continue to *live* like she was going to be ok. We were sent home to await the results.

A sigh of relief left our bodies when the call came, but it was cancer, a rare blood cancer called Waldenstrom Macroglobulinemia. The next part is what hit me the hardest: it was an incurable rare blood cancer, a disease that would eventually take her life. I excused myself to the hall bathroom and quickly locked the door behind me. I stared into the mirror trying not to cry, trying to be strong like Cindy was. I just asked God, WHY? Why her? Why now? After all the adversity in getting Kam back, why was this happening? I couldn't quit, but my heart was breaking. It took me almost fifty years to find the love of my life, why was He taking her away? What could be the lesson in that? But there was one. I had learned self-love, acceptance, perseverance, and that life was way bigger than just me. Now, I would be shown the power of a warrior's mindset: to believe it, to speak it, and to live it. I dried my eyes and made my way down the hall back to my wife. There she was with a smile. She took my hands and consoled me saying, "It's ok, Babe. I will live, not die." She was the one that, out of nowhere, had been diagnosed with an incurable blood cancer yet was still encouraging and loving me unconditionally. I was about to find out just how much awesome sauce my wife was made of.

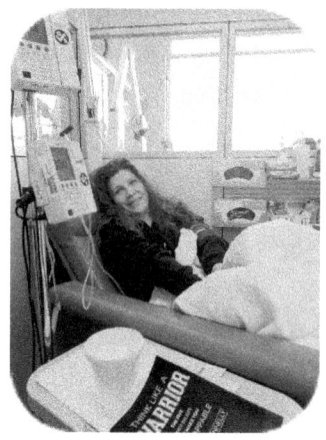

I will live; I will not die.

It was such a whirlwind. She had surgery to put in a port to receive medication. The following week, she began her chemo treatments. She would be in for two days a month for six months. It seemed like one day, we were in the Smoky Mountains, and the next, she was receiving infusions of chemo at the cancer center. I was grateful that the infusions did not make her sick, just a little tired, and they didn't make her lose her long, beautiful, curly, brown hair. I accompanied her to all her treatments and appointments over the next six months. She had my back; I had to have hers. As we came to the middle of the six months there began to be improvement in her blood work numbers. Each month they became drastically better. During this whole experience she never let fear show through. She never spoke of anything but living and not dying. I had a front row seat to the mindset of a warrior woman that impacts me to this day. I am sure that silently, in her alone time, she had to have experienced fear; she had to wonder *what if*. But she never showed it, and I never saw it. All I ever witnessed was that she believed she would live; she had work to do. She only spoke of a complete healing and a long future with me. Most importantly, her actions showed it. She lived that mindset, in all she did.

A warrior's mindset

At the end of the treatment she was considered in complete remission. Her cancer check-up appointments are now every six months instead of every three. Her blood work continues to show her to be as healthy as she ever was. She believes she is cancer free, even though, medically, it is called remission. They say it will eventually return. Who knows if that is true? All I know is that I was taught the warrior's mindset by my wife. As educators, we must acquire that weapon for our arsenal. Adversity comes at us from every direction on a minute by minute basis. As educators, we know all too well that life never stops throwing us left hooks and sucker punches. Having the power of a warrior's mindset makes a difference in our effectiveness. It enhances our ability to connect and build relationships. In life, we are either in the midst of adversity, coming out of a period of adversity, or about to go through another storm. When we see all that is right, instead of all that is wrong, we keep the needle on our mindset meter towards the positive. When we *believe* we can, we *say* we can and *live* like we can then, we can. A warrior's mindset will grow us through all we go through as educators. In all things – good, bad, and ugly – believe it, speak it, and live it. I walk into school each morning with that mindset. A room full of sixth graders is a piece of cake compared to cancer. My wife looked death in the face with a smile and said, "I will live; I will not die." Cindy Lou Who, I love you. Thank you for teaching me all about the next ingredient in that secret sauce – a warrior's mindset.

CHAPTER EIGHT
The Gift of Grace

We have talked about self-love, acceptance, perseverance, and mindset. These all require discipline, development, and dedication. But there is one ingredient you can add to your recipe instantly. While it still needs discipline, development, and dedication, you can begin using it now: Grace. The power of a simple act of forgiveness is underrated and often misunderstood but will bring immediate peace to your personal life and calm the chaos of being an educator. It just takes a little humility and intentionality to learn why it is needed to take your teaching, profession, or relationship to the next level.

I always thought that asking for forgiveness and giving grace were things that absolved a wrong. In reality, they are something totally different. They allow us to guard against resentment. They remove the need to hold a grudge while keeping us peacefully focused on building real, authentic relationships. I learned this lesson when I was encouraged to ask forgiveness from someone that I felt needed to be doing the asking. Why did I need to ask for forgiveness? I didn't need grace, they did. Today, I embrace when I am wrong because it is an opportunity to learn and bring that secret sauce to the next level of savory excellence.

One day, I was sitting in my coaches' office after practice. I was talking to my assistant coach, AJ, about the team, church, and life in general. He was the one who had encouraged me to get back into coaching. I had given up one of my biggest passions because it had cut into my drinking time, but his prodding got me back to doing one of the things I do best. I had one condition when I applied. If I got the job, AJ would become my assistant coach. He was a young kid, a former Division I player, and I had coached against him when he was a teen. We shared a love for the game of soccer, a quest for the truth about God and love, and he was also the pastor at the church I was attending. We were becoming good friends and would often spend time talking man to man about our dreams and where we were headed with the purpose we both knew was inside us. I can't recall why AJ and I even began to talk about my dad's and my relationship that day after practice, but I shared with him that my relationship with my dad had been excruciatingly painful for me for a long time. The hole that was left in me from early on was beginning to fill during my recovery, and a large part of it was due to the fact that my dad was also recovering. Our relationship was coming full circle; he was becoming my hero again. Over the years, he had asked for forgiveness many times, and for the longest time, I did all I could to punish him. It was at that point that my assistant coach asked me a question, "Have you ever asked your dad for forgiveness?"

I was immediately offended. What the heck did I have to ask him to forgive? *He* needed *my* grace; I surely didn't need his. But as we continued to talk, I began to make more sense of what he was trying to say. Sure, my dad had hurt me; he broke my heart. But as I stepped back and reflected on my life, I was reminded that I was in no position to judge anyone. I had broken many hearts. My first wife, my children, my parents, I had let most of the people who loved me down in a huge way. As we talked, I began to feel the guilt and remorse that my dad must have felt. I could see I had to own the resentment for him that I still had inside me. AJ told me that to really be free from it, all I needed was to ask for his forgiveness for the way I had treated him for so long. I kept him away from my kids, left him out of family milestones and holidays, all in an attempt to punish him for his past mistakes. That to be able to receive grace I had to be able to remove the unforgiveness from my heart. It almost seemed backwards, but it could not have been more true. For me to be able to give grace, especially to the ones who really need it, like my students, I had to receive it by removing all resentment and grudges that I held suppressed deep down in my soul. So, my assistant coach gave me a directive, "Go home right now, call your dad, and ask for his forgiveness for how you have treated him. You will be amazed at the gift grace will bring to your heart and how it will open you up to give that grace back freely, especially to the ones who don't deserve it." We wrapped it up, said our goodbyes for the day, and I headed home to do just what he had asked me to do.

I drove home, still curious why asking my dad for forgiveness would even matter. Our relationship was on the rebound, and we had grown from the past. But something inside me was pushing me home to make that call; it was like that secret sauce was calling for another ingredient lesson. Once I got home, I put away my keys and backpack, grabbed my phone, and dialed my dad's number. His always pleasant voice was on the other end, "Hello, my son. I am glad you called." I just went right into it, my voice cracking with emotion. I told my father that I was sorry for always keeping him at arm's length, for punishing him for his mistakes in the past by keeping my children away from him. I apologized for slighting him during the holidays in favor of everyone else. I said, "Dad, I am asking for your grace and your forgiveness for all that I have done to punish you since the divorce with Mom." There was a small period of silence. Then, he just came back with, "Son, you do not know how much that means to me, and I forgave you a long time ago." I could instantly feel a weight physically lift off of me. Finally, I could sense our relationship had been not just restored but reborn. What would come back to me in asking for grace from my Dad would be the lesson my secret sauce was needing me to learn.

My dad, the superhero   *My dad and me*

In asking for forgiveness from my dad, I was reminded of all the times forgiveness and grace had been extended to me. There were too many times for me to count. Yet, my heart was also relieved of all the guilt, shame, and resentment it held in regard to the relationship between my dad and me. My hero was back. The gift of calm and peace I felt was infinite. The past was laid to rest, and I could clearly see the path forward. Grace drove out all forms of hate and replaced it with an unlimited supply of unconditional love. That is the key. When we give grace, when we ask for forgiveness, it is great for those who accept it. But the gift it gives us is a necessary ingredient in our secret sauce. The tranquility of unconditional love that we need to become the educators we were called to be for our students' and staff's needs. The gift of grace raises our ability to build authentic relationships and connections to life-changing levels. It keeps the focus off of ourselves and on loving and leading students and staff to believe and discover that they are the greatest miracle in the world. In that call with my father, a miracle happened. I was freed of my past. We were freed of our past, and that freedom allowed us to re-create the most beautiful father-son relationship. The gift of grace allows us, as educators, to give heaping doses of unconditional love in our schools, and that is an ingredient in that secret sauce our students, staff, communities, and society desperately needs.

Forgiveness, the gift of grace, is so often misunderstood. For the longest time, I had it backwards: it was all for me, not for the other person. If I did wrong, I was to ask for forgiveness, and it would take away the mistake. If someone did me wrong, I was to extend grace allowing me to be the bigger person. You see, I thought the gift of grace was all about me, yet I have learned that it is actually for others. The miracle in this gift is what it returns to you when you humbly ask for it and unconditionally give it. Sure, my dad felt better after I humbly owned the wrong I had put on him, but it returned the gift of grace *to* me, not *for* me. I received a peaceful serenity with unconditional love that I could then extend and give away freely to others, especially in my classroom and on the soccer field. Grace gives us a freedom as educators that isn't for us but given to us so that we can pass it on to the multitudes we serve. They cry out for acceptance and unconditional love, and when we live in the practice of giving and asking for grace, our mindset is shifted to where the focus needs to be, on why we got into education in the first place. Just like our secret sauce, that gift of grace only becomes a power for us when we realize it isn't a gift we are to keep to ourselves but one we must give away freely to all those faces in front of us each day. They just need to know that someone cares enough to say, "The past is the past; let's move forward." When we are trying to develop as educators, the opportunity to fail exists, but our staff needs to know that we are still seen, heard, and valued. Grace does just that. It brings schools together as a real team. It ignites the attitude of we over me, and frees us to focus on serving. The gift of grace is a part of that secret sauce that releases us to cook up all kinds of greatness. Give it, receive it, and remember, it isn't for you to keep, but the power that comes back to you will enable you to change the lives of many.

CHAPTER NINE
Reaching Back Over the Mountain

Discovering our secret sauce unlocks the mystery of our purpose. Finding that secret sauce was not a milestone of success for my personal glory or accolades; it was so that my life would become the game changer it was designed to be for others. Once we understand and begin to develop the necessary ingredients, the only way to release its magic is to serve it up. We do that by putting into practice all those ingredients so that we learn to cook them up in a way that allows us to build relationships that leave a positive, lasting impact. Our secret sauce is something we are always developing, yet always serving for the empowerment of others. All those mountains we climbed, all those times we went to hell and back, become the power of our story only when we reach back over the mountain and into the darkness of hell to pull others through to the other side. That is what our secret sauce is all about, that is the miracle in our why.

As educators, we serve every single day. We serve other people's kids, our staff, our school, and our community in many ways that go unseen and are seldom appreciated. One of the important lessons I have learned through serving up that secret sauce is that we are not measured by what we get but what we give. In our society, it is the exact opposite, which is why this is one of the hardest things to pass along to our students and staff. Today, it is all about who has the most stuff to be envious of – the biggest house, the nicest car. That is value and status in America, and it is also one big lie. When all is said and done, it is never about how much we have, but rather how well we gave what we did have away. Of all those secret sauce gifts we all possess, did we keep them to ourselves, or did we freely pass them out to all who needed them? As a teacher, a coach, or an administrator, one of the best lessons we can teach those we serve is that our relationships, those connections and bonds we forge, become life-altering when we realize it is all about what we give and not about what we get. One of the values instilled into the team I coach is that we are not measured by a record or a scoreboard, but rather by what we gave to the team in the process. We serve to give, not to get rewarded for it. Every day we do this, we win the heart lottery. We never walk out the doors to go home without the prize of knowing we made a difference.

When I got back into coaching soccer at Sapulpa High School in Sapulpa, OK, it was the perfect chance to put my secret sauce into action. I was taking on a team that was full of adversity and devoid of culture and a winning mindset. This would prove not to be adversity but my advantage in developing that secret sauce. During my four-year tenure there I was able to not only believe and speak it, I was able to live it out. The fruits of putting my heart and soul into young people, serving them that secret sauce, were that I got to see it unfold right in front of my eyes. Just by being of service, just by giving that secret sauce away, I was finally able to see the gifts that I had been given. Even on the hardest days, I find peace and fulfillment knowing that I reached back over the mountain I had climbed and helped someone on their way to the summit. For those four years, every day, I practiced the ingredients of my secret sauce. It was uncomfortable, but I was able to grow and become more disciplined in giving away my time, myself, and my love to others. I hadn't gone to hell and back for nothing; I made it back so I could become a sherpa to others searching for a way out of the hell they found themselves in.

All in and all together

One aspect of being an educator and a coach I had always been blind to was the act of service. Being a soccer coach not only gave me an opportunity to learn how to serve, it taught me the importance of service in using that secret sauce. Going the second mile, all in and all together with grit, was the exact recipe that allowed my secret sauce to become top-notch effective in building relationships that impacted the trajectory of the lives of my players, the parents, and the school community. It was the glue bonding us together, not just as a brotherhood but as a family as true as I have ever experienced. Becoming the head boys' soccer coach at Sapulpa High School was the proving ground for how blessed I was to have had the life experiences that helped me find my secret sauce. Sharing my story became real and intentional, and by weaving it into the fabric of my coaching, the culture of that program was transformed. I finally believed in myself, and in turn, I could pass that belief along to my team, rent free, until they could find their own. I felt like I was the hero in one of those happy-ever-after sports movies. Coaching that team was the best feeling I had ever felt in my professional life. I found my purpose: to love and lead kids like Aiden, Carson, Tyson, Caleb, Jaxon, Nick, Tanner, Spencer, TJ, Trey, Connor, Kendall, Colton, and Keefer to believe and discover that they were the greatest miracles in the world. There were others too, but the two that really stuck with me and that allowed me to reach back over that mountain were Mason and Nate Sarver. They were twins and knuckleheads but were also two young men who unlocked in me that unlimited potential to serve up my secret sauce that was a game changer for me and those I will serve for the rest of my life.

When I first met Mason and Nate, they reminded me so much of my own sons, Blake and Brady. They were full of life, ornery, mischievous, and had been to their own hell and back, just like my boys. I could see the miracle inside them both, fighting to break out. My sons deserved better from me, and they didn't get that until much later in their life. This was my opportunity to honor Blake and Brady by leading and loving these two boys. They didn't make it easy, and there were times I doubted I would ever connect with them on a level that would make a real difference. However, that never stopped me from having the mindset of a warrior. *Try harder, Daddy,* and that look in my sons' eyes the night I told them I was leaving their mother wouldn't have let me give up on Mason and Nate if I had wanted to.

The first year of coaching Mason and Nate was fulfilling and frustrating all at the same time. Both of the boys were talented but could not get out of their own way. Mason was projected early on to be my starting center back, yet he doubted himself at every turn, which came out as tantrums against my staff and me. I could see he wanted to succeed so badly, but he never really believed he deserved it. Nate was more aloof, worked as hard as he had to and no more. He just had a good time; sometimes, way too much of a good time. Nate would end up being a starter that first year, but he held back from really going all in. Mason would play on the junior varsity team, struggling all year long to believe the miracle that I saw. These two boys had a hard exterior to get through, and rightfully so. Life had not been an easy ride for either of them. Their anger at the world and their home lives would show up in practices. Their behavior had my assistant coach pushing me to kick them off the team. I remember that conversation like it was yesterday. "AJ," I said, "not only are these two boys going to be great, they are on my account, and I will never quit on them. And by the way Coach, we are going to win ten games and go to the playoffs." He just looked at me, shook his head like I was crazy, and said, "OK, but you deal with Mason and Nate." God gave me Mason and Nate; they were a blessing to me. The secret sauce that I had felt for so long in my soul was about to come alive like the eruption of Mt. Vesuvius. The life-changing energy would electrify that locker room, that program, that team, those twin boys and me.

We wound up heading into the last game with a record of ten wins and four losses. It looked like a lock to get into the playoffs. We were in a three-way tie for the final two spots and held the advantage in most of the tiebreakers. We struggled during the junior varsity game, and Mason had a meltdown. He was taken out of the game and refused to go back in. As we prepared for the varsity match, Mason refused to take part. He sat off by himself, hood on his head, and he would not speak to me. After trying to talk him off the ledge, I had to get back to the team and prepare. It broke my heart each time he didn't respond. I wanted so badly to connect with him, for him to have this miraculous breakthrough, but what I didn't realize was that the seed had been planted. We ended up losing that game 2 to 1 and ended the season with a 10 and 5 record. The team had gone from two wins the year before to 10 wins in just one season. They were starting to believe that they were champions, they were beginning to carry themselves as champions, on and off the field. We would end up with a dose of Murphy's law in the tie-break system and be on the outside looking in as the playoffs went on without us. But the change that was occurring in those boys and myself was nothing short of a miracle. That secret sauce was in full force because I understood how to serve. The return on my investment of love and time was transforming my heart too. I knew I had changed, my life was turning around, but this team and our experience together was showing me just how great that change was. I had only one regret, Mason. I would not leave him behind; I would find a way to bring him and Nate right along with me.

The next year, Mason and Nate's senior season, wasn't as special on the field as our first year together, but it bonded us together in an unbreakable way. Those boys finally saw that I really loved them, and I would not stop leading them to be their best selves. Mason became team captain, they both became starters, and even earned All-State honorable mention recognition. They led together on the field. They didn't quit in practice, they gave me all they had in games, and they were finding family, as we all were. You see, our secret sauce has a way of instilling a belief in those we serve that they really can dream big as well as achieve their dreams. They find purpose and real, authentic connection. Those things open them up to a world full of opportunities instead of obstacles. And because I would not quit on Mason and Nate, it forged a relationship, and they would not quit on me either. On senior night, I could barely speak when it came to them. Heck, I am crying as I write this story. Those two boys taught me how to be a real game changer. Mason and Nate, helped me see the success of sharing my secret sauce. They finished their playing careers that night with a win and the hugs those two gave me after the game brought us all to tears. I had never seen Nate cry, but that night as he hugged me he cried like a baby. However, my time with them wasn't over. Mason and Nate might have graduated and finished as players for my team, but those Sarver boys and I belonged together.

*Reach back over that mountain
(Nate Sarver, Me, Mason Sarver)*

Mason wound up becoming my assistant coach the next year. He went from a kid everyone else wanted kicked off the team, to the best assistant I have ever had. Mason went from a punk kid to an incredible young man I was proud to call family. Those boys have been the two I could always count on. To many, it seemed odd because they were the ones our society easily overlooked, but I saw them. Mason and I became especially close. This 19-

year-old kid made my beard turn gray. Then, two years later, I now turned to him for advice on all things related to coaching the team. I trusted his insight. Not only had I reached back over that mountain for him, he grabbed hold of me and didn't let go. Our secret sauce is funny like that. When we go all in, serving and going that second mile in building relationships, miracles happen. Connections are formed that open up those we serve to all they ever dreamed they could be. Bonds are created that not only alter their lives but powerfully change our own. It is why we do what we do. When we reach back over that mountain and bring others to the summit and down the other side to a life of promise, a really magical thing happens. They begin to reach back over that mountain and grab hold of more souls lost in a hell like they knew. I was honored to get a front row seat to see Mason do this for many of our younger players who were in a struggle he knew all too well. When we pass on that secret sauce and plant those seeds, we never really know when and how they might grow. There will be more Masons out there, Nates too. That is our legacy as educators. When we commit like we are in a room with no exit to serve those we lead and love, they soon believe and discover that they too are the greatest miracles in the world. They start loving and leading others to do the same. Your secret sauce is your superpower. Never take it for granted; always look to serve. There are Masons and Nates who need you, who need that secret sauce. Mason and Nate, if you ever read this, I love you both.

CHAPTER TEN
Dream big, so big they call you crazy.

Dreaming big is an important ingredient to top off that secret sauce within you. When building relationships and establishing connections and culture within our classrooms and schools, dreaming big is vital. Many of our students and staff have given up on big dreams, especially since March 2020, when Covid hit the world. During that time, most people went into survival mode and stayed inside their comfortable bubbles. To the heck with big dreams; just give me what I need to stay afloat. Our students need us to model big dreams again. We can't model this if we don't ever take risks and show them the empowerment that comes from dreaming big. We need high expectations and to set our goals high. Then, we need to get in the arena with our students and staff and fight tooth and nail alongside them, get bruised and bloody, as we pursue those lofty goals each and every day. And in doing battle with them, ignore the critics. The bigger the dream, the more people will call you crazy.

What is the point of forming relationships and creating connections, if we don't use the power in those bonds to raise the level our schools believe they can reach? We can tell them, we can cheer them on, but if you want your secret sauce to do the magic it is capable of, you must dream big. You must show them. In 2021, I dreamed a dream so big that most people thought I really was crazy. It scared the dickens out of me, but dreaming big was the best move I have ever made. It wasn't just a cute catch phrase; it was that perfect topping to my secret sauce. I lived it, revealing how the relationships and connections we have in our lives are the support and push to making those big dreams our reality. They become the stories we use to motivate and encourage others that not only can they dream big again, but those big dreams absolutely can come true.

We each have our own unique blend of ingredients to our secret sauce, how we share our stories to impact others. But before we begin a school year, a month, a week, even a day, we must have a vision of what we want to accomplish by building relationships. We must be willing to take great risks and become extremely uncomfortable if we are truly going to inspire those around us to do the same. If we are not inspiring others to greatness, then we are just the flavor of the month, full of inspiration to mediocrity. I talked about dreaming big all the time. I dreamed of winning a state championship, of being the educator I needed when I was in school, of writing this book and making the Secret Sauce a real business; however, I did more talking than doing. Yet once I stepped way outside my comfort zone and took risks people thought I was crazy to take, dreaming big became living those big dreams in real time. To unlock the unlimited potential of my secret sauce that had been bursting through since my recovery, I needed to stop talking about big dreams and do big things that led me to the place of my dreams. Work only comes after success in the dictionary. Therefore, I needed to act to unleash the superpower within that secret sauce. If I wanted others to dream big, I had to dream big first.

During the Covid pandemic, my eyes were opened to the fact that although I was trying to make a difference and focus on my purpose, I was beholden to the paycheck and its necessity in order to survive. Sure, we have to take care of our financial responsibilities, but we let those lull us to sleep. Then, all we have left are dreams that are not realistic because we have bills to pay and our responsibilities cannot afford big risks or being outside that comfort zone. It was during this time that I began to question many things. Were we living just to pay the bills and keep a roof over our heads or were we really living? Could we be locked in this mundane cycle, going round and round until we meet the end and die? I wanted to *live* big dreams, not just *talk* about them. So, we began to talk about moving. Cindy and I had frequently vacationed in the Woodland Park, Colorado area. We fell in love with the area so much that we had decided to move there once we retired. Why wait till we retire? Is there a perfect time? What if we never make it to retirement? We decided we didn't want to live with a bunch of what ifs. We wanted to dream big, so big they called us crazy – then, make that big dream our reality.

We were Oklahoma natives, living there for over 45 years. Packing up and moving to a small mountain town sounded like a pipe dream. It was a move that went way beyond any comfort zone; it was terrifying. Change is daunting enough, but I had been prepared to take such risks. If I could go from being a homeless alcoholic to a recovering educator living his why, then I could do this. Cindy, however, took a little more coaxing. Our past experiences didn't define us as an addict and a cancer survivor, but it did make us look at life in a way we had not before. Each day, each breath, was precious, and we could not see wasting any more days or breaths. We were moving to the mountains. They were calling, and we were going. However, if it were not for the deep relationship shared between my wife and me, I don't think we ever could have done it. We were the push and the encouragement the other needed to make this big dream happen. But dreaming big requires a plan broken into smaller goals with a timeline, so you stop talking about it and actually do it.

We needed a plan. We set timelines for selling our home and buying a new one. Employment would need to be secured and trips to the mountains needed to be scheduled to search for a home to buy there. With just several months to get it all done, we set the plan and started taking massive steps of action leading with faith over the fear we were experiencing. I have heard it said that anything great does not come easy. While this is true, the reward is so much more than you can imagine. Around the time of spring break in 2021 there was a position posted for teaching social studies at Woodland Park Middle School. Although I was in the midst of a soccer season, I jumped at the chance. I got on the phone with the principal at the high school, Kevin Burr, and the now-former superintendent of schools, Steve Woolf, and let them know that we were coming this time. Two strong connections I was developing that would help guide me through the transition and encourage me to share that secret sauce in the Woodland Park School District. I got an interview a few weeks later and was eventually offered the position. I never even asked about the pay scale, I just said YES, a million times YES. It was the leap of faith that began the process of turning this big dream into an even bigger reality. There was no turning back now. Cindy was working remotely at the time and could continue to do so. We both had jobs – one goal accomplished.

In May of 2021, we contacted a realtor friend of ours to come look at the house so that we could get it ready to sell. We shared with her that we wanted to list it at the end of the month so that everything would be in place. She came out and toured our home, gave us a list of things to do, and got all the paperwork arranged so that the listing would be active at the end of May. The next week we got a call that she had a friend with a family who was interested in looking at our house. Good grief! We didn't even have it listed or staged and ready to show yet. We agreed to let her show them the home without really thinking much of it. The showing exploded into an offer that we just could not refuse. There were some kinks to work out in the contract, but we had taken another huge step outside our comfort zone and basically had an agreement to sell our home before we had even listed it. We had lived in Oklahoma almost our entire lives, and our house sold in just a few days. Now what? We had no home in Colorado. Where were we going to live?

Another goal bit the dust, but now we had several more obstacles to tackle. At the end of May we spent a week up in Woodland Park looking for our next home. We had to be out of our house in Oklahoma by mid-June, so time was of the essence. The housing market in the mountains was crazy. Prices were sky high, and people were paying cash for way over listing price. It was like trying to find that proverbial needle in a haystack. We also looked at the lone apartment complex in town, but a third-story, two-bedroom was $2,000 a month, and with two big dogs, was not an ideal option. We even looked into buying a tiny home, convinced we could do it, but looking back we were so glad that fell through because we probably would not have liked living literally on top of one another. We had started this process with faith over fear, yet fear was pulling alongside making it a tight race. The connection we shared brought us through. There were many times, with one of us crying, that one had to remind the other that we believed it would work out, we spoke it, and we lived it, even if one had to hold the other up. Relationships are cool like that. When we have those real authentic connections in our life, we are never fighting in the arena alone.

We were back and forth from Colorado to Oklahoma the next couple of months. We spent June and July living in hotels in Tulsa and in Woodland Park. The night before our last trip back to Oklahoma, we submitted an offer on a home. It was July 1st and time was running out. We met the realtor on the way out of town to give her our earnest money check. We held out hope, but every offer we had made that summer was declined because someone would out bid us with cash. We believed, we spoke, and we beat back the fear with faith as we headed out that morning. As we pulled into the hotel parking lot in Tulsa some ten hours later, we got a call. Our offer was accepted; we had a home. We would move into the house on August the 2nd. We were ecstatic that we only had to live in a motel for another month and started planning for inspections and moving all of our stuff from the storage units to Colorado. It was a whirlwind, but faith over fear let the excitement of dreaming big lead us. It was really happening. We were living big, full of intention and purpose, and we both had never felt so alive.

At the end of July, the relationships and connections I had established with my team at Sapulpa would show the benefit of just how powerful a culture built in love really is. I had rented the largest U-Haul truck available and needed help loading everything. We had two large storage units full of everything we owned, and that was after downsizing quite a bit. My assistant coach Mason and his brother Nate, the twins who I had grown so close to, worked for Mayflower moving, what a miracle that was. I put the word out for help and was overwhelmed at what came back to me. All that effort we had put into building a family in that soccer program had paid off. Parents, current players, and alumni all showed up to help get us loaded. We had the twenty-six-foot moving truck professionally packed and loaded in under three hours. I was so moved by the outpouring of love there that day. It was 110 on the heat index, but that didn't stop them from showing up and pouring back into their coach. I could not have done it without them. Dreaming big was made possible by sharing that secret sauce and developing life changing connections and relationships. My time with that program had come to an end, but they sent me to the mountains with a love you can only know when you go all in with those you serve. As they drove away and I sat in the cab of that U-Haul, it hit me. My secret sauce was not about me, but what it paid back to me when I gave it away was priceless. I have family like I've never known with those boys and parents. Those relationships have changed me forever, and their love empowered me to live out what I always told them. Dream big, so big they call you crazy.

We made it.

We pulled our U-Haul up to our new home on August the second in Woodland Park, Colorado. We had made it. The plans and timelines we had set helped us get there. The connections and relationships we had formed made it possible. We were greeted that afternoon by the Athletic Director from Woodland Park and the high school football team. They had the contents of that truck unloaded and into our new home in one hour. I never had to carry one thing inside. We were looking out our master bedroom window; Cindy and I just stared at Pikes

Peak in awe. If this was a dream, pinch me. She did, and it hurt. This was really happening, we were breathing in the smell of pine and mountain air, while viewing the most majestic of earth's creations. Dreaming big had led us to living big. All that we had been through, together and separately, in our pasts had become our story. Our story and experiences had developed in us that secret sauce necessary in living big on purpose. We were loving others and leading them to believe and discover that they were the greatest miracle in the world. It was becoming enmeshed into the fabric of everything we did. We took big risks and stepped way outside of our comfort zone. Together we were seeing just how intentional sharing that secret sauce could be and how incredibly alive it made us feel. We spent years letting the process of our lives develop and discipline us to make a difference. Dreaming big was the cherry on top. It was the last ingredient that gave us clarity into just how powerful that secret sauce could be. You need to live a life that you dream of, a life that bears the fruit of you being the greatest miracle in the world. There is no perfect time; stop making that excuse. It all comes down to you making the choice to take risks and getting outside your little bubble of comfort. Let's go; let's make a difference. Let's dream big, so big they call us crazy.

CONCLUSION

So, there you have it, the secret sauce. Our life experiences, our education career, and our story, combined with all the tough and necessary lessons, become the ingredients that make up our secret sauce. We all have it; it's right there inside us. Educators everywhere need to believe and discover that power and magic within themselves. The young people of our world desperately need a mega dose of that secret sauce. And our staff needs a shot of it to relight the fire that brought them to the profession in the first place. Teaching, coaching, and leading is your platform to share that secret sauce within you. As a community of educators we must get back to going all in and being all together.

When I was in the darkest places of my alcoholism, I would have laughed at anyone preaching the message of being the greatest miracle in the world. But what I know now is that through all that darkness was the chance to grow if I could just put myself and all my troubles aside to see it. If we make a stand and hit our lives head-on, we can get through all of the different types of darkness we face. For me, it took hitting rock bottom. I don't wish that for anyone, but my mindset shifted from me to we. I began to see that my story, especially the ugly parts, was meant to be shared, and developing the ingredients to that secret sauce would allow me to do that effectively. In no way has it been easy. There are days even now when it is almost too much, but I remember that I GET TO. My obstacles are opportunities. My adversity becomes my advantage in reaching back over the mountain to help students and staff climb to the summit.

During the selfish time of my life, I wanted to make a difference, but I had no idea how. When I lost my baby girl, the last thing I had left, I realized that my life was not about me but what I could do with it to serve others. That opened the door to me being able to uncover and refine that secret sauce within me. It was the beginning of a new life and a fresh start in becoming the teacher and coach I knew I was supposed to be. My why: to lead and love students and staff to believe and discover that they are the greatest miracle in the world, only became clear when my mindset shifted from me to we. The life I wanted, the educator I wanted to be, could only become my reality when I stopped saying WHY ME and started saying WHY NOT ME.

Your secret sauce evolves as your story continues, one day at a time. Your adversity, your struggles, your wins and celebrations only add to the flavor. The story that is unfolding in front of you, combined with your natural gifts and abilities are what I call that secret sauce. Your secret sauce is disciplined and developed by specific ingredients that we are taught through the ups and downs of our story. For me, it was ingredients like self-love, acceptance, perseverance, mindset, grace, service, and grit. These ingredients are what taught me the importance and power within my story and gave me the ability to build authentic relationships.

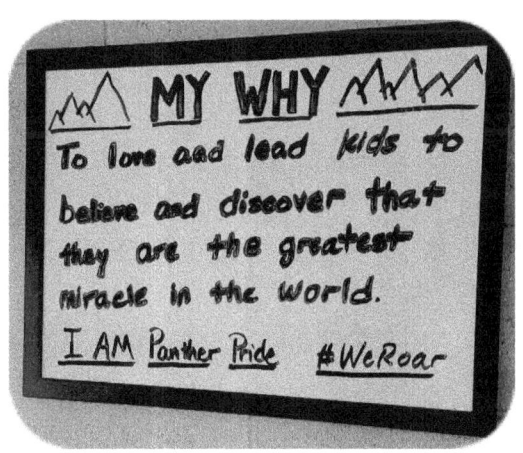

My WHY hangs in my classroom.

You may think you have no story, no secret sauce. I hate to break it to you, but you are wrong. If you step back from yourself and look at all the good you do as an educator, you will find some clarity and begin your process of developing your unique secret sauce. You don't teach for you, do you? Lean into the reason you get up everyday and go into your school. I have shared mine with you, and I do that through building real, authentic relationships with those I serve. I encourage you to reflect on your reason, your why, then write it down. I challenge you to display it in your classroom, and refer to it often. This has created many opportunities for me to share my why with my students and staff. Being an educator is *what* I do. Being an author, speaker, teacher, and a coach is *how* I do it. My why is my purpose for living, and it makes me feel more alive today than I have ever felt in my life.

I believe education is in a state of flux, sometimes chaos, in our country. We need educators like you to know your why and share your story. Dive into the lessons the ingredients in your life are trying to teach you and become vulnerable. Show those you serve your authentic self. Share how you have overcome obstacles and turned them into opportunities. There are so many of us going through tremendous storms – financial difficulties, divorces, relationship failures, health scares, and even addiction. Throw that on top of the day-to-day difficulties of being an educator, and it is obvious why so many promising game changers are leaving this profession. Turning that adversity into your advantage not only brings empowerment and healing to yourself, it will bring the same to many students and staff who have or are going through the same thing. You can overcome any obstacle; you just have to believe you can. Then, never, ever, ever, quit. Let the lessons in your struggles become the ingredients to refine that secret sauce. There are many who look to you that need exactly what you have to offer.

I challenge you to see all that is right, not all that is wrong. Realize that this life is not about us, but about how we can lead and love others. You may feel like your life has little meaning, but your story matters. Look around you at all those kids and fellow educators who look to you for love and leadership. That is the beginning of understanding that you too are the greatest miracle in the world. I know I matter today because I have a secret sauce that could literally be a game changer for someone else. Even if it is just one person. I have learned that when you don't quit, you win. And all the trips to hell and back really matter when I reach back over those mountains with an outstretched hand to pull people out of their own hell and back to the summit. With so much hopelessness in our profession, our stories need to be told. Our secret sauce needs to be shared. If not us, then who? So, instead of saying why me, join me; and say why not me.

ACKNOWLEDGEMENTS

Finding my secret sauce would not have been possible without the love and support of people who reached back over that mountain to help pull me up.

I want to thank my counselor at Valley Hope Recovery Center in Cushing, Oklahoma, Christie Hamner, for getting me started on my own road to awesome and finding my secret sauce. She was instrumental in me making the choice to change my life. I also want to thank my roommate at Valley Hope, Aaron Triplett, who was a huge influence on my road to recovery. And last but not least, Mary and Hoyt Hyden, who breathed life into this dream of mine. My recovery from alcoholism was the foundation for this book.

I must acknowledge the following people from my education family. Without their love and support I do not think I would be here today. Cecil Bowles, Gayla Sewell, Shelly Lansdale, Lisa Corn, Ann Eichenberger, Jason Parker, Kevin Burr, Erin Street, and Yvonne Goings. As educators we become family. These people loved me when I was not very lovable. I will be forever in your debt and grateful that you have added such love to my secret sauce.

From my world of soccer, a game that has always given me a platform to excel and now give back to others in a great way, I must acknowledge the following people: Coaches Jim Ainsworth and Nathan Shotts, who were my surrogate belief when I did not believe in myself; AJ Klerekoper, who was the catalyst to get me back into coaching after my recovery; Scott Ryan, who was the driving force for me to discover my secret sauce as a coach. And to all my former players and assistant coaches, but especially Mason and Nate Sarver, who showed me how powerful it was to reach back over that mountain.

A huge shout out to Steve Woolf and his Wild Heart Teacher organization. Thank you, from the bottom of my heart, for always being an encourager and giving me a platform to begin sharing my struggle to strength. You have modeled for me what it means to rise by lifting others.

To my mentors and coaches, Darrin Peppard and Brandon Beck: you two not only opened my eyes to this reality but set me on a course, kept me on track and challenged me to make this dream come true. I am a better man and educator because of your wisdom, influence, and guidance. I will continue to unlock unlimited potential on my road to awesome.

And last, thank you to my family. Without my kids, my mom, my dad and Marcie, and my wife Cindy this book would have never been written. They have been the inspiration, the substance, and the heart that has gone into writing this book. These people are the greatness that is within me and this book was written as a testament to all you have been to me. I wanted to die, but because of all of you, I chose to live. My wish is that it honors you all, forever and always.

ABOUT THE AUTHOR

Having almost thirty years' experience in education, Kip is sharing his secret sauce as an educator, coach, author, speaker, and as host of the podcast The Secret Sauce with Kip Shubert. Kip is fierce in his belief that our school's culture and success depends on us being all in and all together in cultivating connections that ensures all stakeholders are seen, heard and valued.

Kip is a proud father of four great kids, three amazing grandchildren and blessed husband to his wife Cindy. He loves to be outdoors, hiking, and especially college football season and Italian food. He is excited to be joining the Road To Awesome family and is grateful that each day he gets to share that secret sauce and make a difference in the lives of staff and students.

BRING KIP TO YOUR COMMUNITY, DISTRICT OR SCHOOL

Kip is a seasoned educator and coach with over three decades of experience. With his empowering style, Kip helps people take their struggles and turn them into strengths, their very own "Secret Sauce," which becomes their superpower in achieving success for students and educators. It is time we tap into that hidden potential within us all and shatter the limitations of traditional education. Invite Kip into your community and together you will reach one another, reach young people, and turn your Struggle to Strength.

Speaking Topics

Struggle To Strength
- Understanding and Discovering Your WHY
- Using the defining moments in your story as your superpower to elevate personal development and academic success with your students
- How to be real, vulnerable, and authentic in developing relationships that leave a legacy

The Real Common Core - Core Values
- Who am I, really? How to find YOU again
- Identifying and aligning our core values

- How to navigate your fears, insecurities, and distractions to be better for yourself and others
- Who are WE, How did WE get here, and Where do WE want to go

A Warrior's Mindset
- 5 steps to establishing a championship culture
- How to cultivate the mindset of a warrior
- How to empower student voice and buy in
- Loving Tough - Being a coach that changes lives

Connect with Kip on social media:
Facebook: Kip Shubert
Twitter: SecretSauceEDU
Instagram: secretsauceedu
LinkedIn: Kip Shubert
YouTube: The Secret Sauce with Kip Shubert
Podcast: The Secret Sauce with Kip Shubert

Email Kip:
teamshu@kipshubert.com

Website:
www.kipshubert.com

MORE BOOKS FROM ROAD TO AWESOME

Taking the Leap: A Field Guide for Aspiring School Leaders by Robert F. Breyer

Transform: Techy Notes to Make Learning Sticky by Debbie Tannenbaum

Becoming Principal: A Leadership Journey & The Story of School Community by Dr. Jeff Prickett

Elevate Your Vibe: Action Planning with Purpose by Lisa Toebben

#OwnYourEpic: Leadership Lessons in Owning Your Voice and Your Story by Dr. Jay Dostal

The Design Thinking, Entrepreneurial, Visionary Planning Leader: A Practical guide for Thriving in Ambiguity by Dr. Michael Nagler

Becoming the Change: Five Essential Elements to Being Your Best Self by Dan Wolfe

inspired: moments that matter by Melissa Wright

Foundations of Instructional Coaching: Impact People, Improve Instruction, Increase Success
by Ashley Hubner

Out of the Trenches: Stories of Resilient Educators
by Dana Goodier

Principled Leader
by Bobby Pollicino

Road to Awesome: The Journey of a Leader
by Darrin Peppard

When Calling Parents Isn't Your Calling: A teacher's guide to communicating with all parents
by Crystal Frommert

CHILDREN'S BOOKS FROM ROAD TO AWESOME

Road to Awesome A Journey for Kids
by Jillian DuBois and Darrin M. Peppard

Emersyn Blake and the Spotted Salamander
by Kim Collazo

Theodore Edward Makes a New Friend
by Alyssa Schmidt

I'm Autistic and I'm Awesome
by Derek Danziger

www.ingramcontent.com/pod-product-compliance
Lightning Source LLC
Chambersburg PA
CBHW072158160426
43197CB00012B/2433